W9-AAL-884

San Rafael High School Library
185 Mission Avenue
San Rafael, CA 94901

THE
FOUR
CORNERS
OF THE
SKY

STEVE ZEITLIN

THE FOUR CORNERS OF THE SKY

CREATION STORIES AND COSMOLOGIES FROM AROUND THE WORLD

PICTURES BY

CHRIS RASCHKA

HENRY HOLT AND COMPANY ✦ NEW YORK

For Amanda, Ben, and Eliza—
the sun, moon, and stars of my cosmos

Acknowledgments
I am deeply indebted to E. C. Krupp, director of the Griffith Observatory in Los Angeles, for reading this manuscript. As he is one of the few individuals on the planet who fully understands both contemporary and ancient astronomy, modern science, and ancient myth, I am awed by the breadth of his knowledge. I also want to thank my wife, folklorist Amanda Dargan, for reading and rereading this book through its many drafts. My editor, Marc Aronson, has been a wonderful collaborator on the project from the outset. Thanks, also, to my fine copyeditor, Deirdre Hare; to my agent, Carla Glasser; to Joseph Bruchac for help with American Indian stories; to Alan Carroll, and Jack Santino; and to ethnomusicologist Lois Wilcken for her help on the section on Haitian Vodou. Finally, thanks to my children, Ben and Eliza, for listening patiently and commenting on many of these stories at the dinner table.

Henry Holt and Company, LLC
Publishers since 1866
115 West 18th Street, New York, New York 10011

Henry Holt is a registered trademark of Henry Holt and Company, LLC
Text copyright © 2000 by Steve Zeitlin
Illustrations copyright © 2000 by Chris Raschka
All rights reserved.
Published in Canada by Fitzhenry & Whiteside Ltd.,
195 Allstate Parkway, Markham, Ontario L3R 4T8.
Library of Congress Cataloging-in-Publication Data
Zeitlin, Steven J. The four corners of the sky:
creation stories and cosmologies from around the world /
Steve Zeitlin; pictures by Chris Raschka.
p. cm.
Summary: A collection of folk stories from around the world,
each accompanied by background information, that explain the various
perspectives of different peoples on how the universe and their world came to be.
1. Cosmology—Folklore. 2. Tales. [1. Cosmology—Folklore. 2. Creation—Folklore.
3. Folklore.] I. Raschka, Christopher, ill. II. Title.
PZ8.1.Z35 Fo 2000 291.2'4—dc21 00-22546

ISBN 0-8050-4816-2 / First Edition—2000
Printed in the United States of America on acid-free paper. ∞
1 3 5 7 9 10 8 6 4 2

Question: My mother is far, far away from me, but every
night we sleep on the same mat and are covered by
the same blanket. What is the mat and what is the
blanket?

Answer: The mat is the earth on which we both sleep,
and the blanket is the sky that covers us all.

—Traditional African riddle, told by Kewulay Kamara

The Brain—is wider than the Sky—
For—put them side by side—
The one the other will contain
With ease—and You—beside

—Emily Dickinson

CONTENTS

THE
FOUR
CORNERS
OF THE
SKY

INTRODUCTION

Imagine yourself in an unfamiliar world. When it is light, a bright orange disk arches across the sky. When it is dark, a silver orb appears amidst thousands of sparkling lights. This glowing silver ball rises and sets at odd hours and varies its shape so that on some nights it appears as a round disk; on others, a half disk, a crescent, a sliver, or it does not appear at all.

This is the world early men and women tried to understand. How could anyone predict when the earth would be light or dark, when the weather would be cold or hot? Would it ever be light or warm again? some must have wondered. How could people measure their days or explain what they saw all around them?

From the early days of humankind, we have watched

the sun rise and set. We have watched the stars come out at night and built our homes amidst the trees, rocks, and hills around us. Yet, each group of people—ancient Egyptians, Babylonians, Jews, Indians, Chinese, Arabs, Africans, Greeks—developed very different pictures of their universe, their *sky-earth* (as the Maya of Guatemala called the world). Many thought of the sun, moon, and stars as Gods, and their movement across the skies as the Gods' glorious journeys.

Using a few basic clues—the cycles of alternating day and night, the cycles of the moon, and the changing length of days and nights—early men and women were able to create a basic calendar. But it took humanity from the dawn of civilization to the seventeenth century, more than four thousand years, to figure out that the earth is round, spins on its axis every twenty-four hours, and revolves around the sun. Ancient cultures believed that the sun moved across the sky, as it appears to do from our spot here on earth. (At evening, we still don't say, "The earth revolved" but rather, "The sun set.") Stories of the Gods explained the world in ways that people could understand.

In a Chinese myth, ten suns crossed the sky each day as glorious, glittering birds. Yi the Archer downed nine of them with his arrows until only one remained.

The ancient Egyptians were fascinated with the way a tiny scarab beetle lays an egg in dung and pushes it around until it becomes a ball—as a result, they sometimes pictured the sun being pushed across the sky by a giant beetle.

In the summer, the Toba-Pilaga Indians, who lived on the border of Paraguay and Argentina, saw the sun as a fat lady, overloaded with the season's bounty, too heavy to move quickly. In winter she lost all her extra pounds and dashed through the sky in shorter and shorter days.

The sky and stars have always been a gigantic funny mirror, a shiny dome in which people see their world reflected—in ways that can help them to understand it.

What Is a Cosmology?

A *cosmology* is a picture of the universe. It names the forces that rule everything around us. A cosmology puts everything in the sky and on the earth into one orderly system. It gives the names for what we call the objects in the sky and enables us to make sense of the universe and our place in it.

A cosmology often includes a *cosmogony*, the story of how everything came to be. No culture is content just to see and describe its universe—we always want to learn where it came from and where it is going. Here are some examples of cosmologies:

The ancient Egyptians believed their universe was a flat island divided in half by a great river, over which hung a heavenly canopy supported by four posts.

The Babylonians thought there were two parts of the universe held together by a cosmic rope.

The early sky lore of ancient India envisioned the earth as a flat disk held up by four elephants that, in turn, were supported by a turtle floating in an eternal sea.

In a myth told by a White Mountain Apache medicine man, the first four people on Earth had to adjust the earth and sun. The earth was too hot, and one of the people said, "The sun is too close to the earth." So they adjusted it to where it is now.

Many Christians envision the world with Heaven above and Hell below. Some believe in Purgatory, a place where people wait before being allowed to enter Heaven.

Until early European explorers and astronomers proved otherwise, many believed that the world was flat and that a person who came too close to the edge would fall off. Some of the writers at the time believed that the earth could not possibly be round, because, in that case, people on the opposite side of the globe would have their head on the ground and their feet up in the air!

In one old story from the *Baba Bathra*, a commentary on the Jewish Talmud, a sacred Hebrew book dating from the year 500 B.C.E., a celebrated Jewish traveler Rabba bar Bar-Hana allowed an Arab to escort him to the edge of the earth. They arrived at the hour of prayer. Before the Jewish traveler prayed, he set his basket of bread down on the horizon, the celestial windowsill. When he finished, he discovered that his basket had vanished. "Who has stolen my bread?" he asked. His escort explained that no one had stolen it but that the wheel of the heavens had turned as he prayed. The next day, sure enough, his bread rose with the sun. His dinner that sank in the west arose as his breakfast in the east.

Our Religion, Their Mythology

In our world, one person's religion is often another's mythology. We think of *ourselves* as having religion, and *others*, mythology. Of course, people a few miles down the road may think about us in the same way. We need to respect the way different groups have tried to make sense of the universe. Many of the cultures in this book are from different historical periods and parts of the world—if you were born into those cultures you would probably think the way they do.

Science has advanced our knowledge of the universe through experimentation. As scientific tools and methods have improved over the centuries, scientists have changed their minds and come up with new theories about the cosmos. Science is not the same as religion or faith. Still, what scientists think is, in part, a reflection of who they are and how they see the world, not just of the world they see.

The myths of a culture are told as true stories. But that doesn't mean that everyone who heard them would swear that they were true. Ancient Greece, for instance, gives us different accounts of how the world was created. In addition, people believe things to different degrees and in different ways. An individual may believe that the universe was created by the "Big Bang," and at the same time believe that God created the world in six days. Ideas that seem contradictory can exist even within the same person's mind.

How This Book Is Organized

For this book I have grouped the world's cosmologies together according to similar themes. So I begin with the cosmologies of the ancient Egyptians and the Maori. Both groups believed the universe was created from world parents who were separated to create the earth and sky. I end with the cosmos of the ancient Chinese and of contemporary science, grouping them together because both universes are thought to have been created from a great burst in space and time—for the Chinese it was P'an Ku's hatching from an egg; for modern scientists it is the Big Bang that created the planets and stars.

For each of the cosmologies in this book, I offer a little background about the culture that created it. For some, I also retell one of the myths that further explains a particular culture's view of the world. A cosmology is not a snapshot of the universe. It is closer to a movie about the cosmos because it changes over time. These world pictures fill in what we can see with stories that go back to the beginning and take us to the end of time.

In his beautiful book *Beyond the Blue Horizon*, the astronomer E. C. Krupp writes, "The sky speaks in celestial objects; the sun, the moon, the planets, and the stars are its vocabulary." Creating a cosmology, telling myths and stories about the sun and stars are among the ways we make this planet home—as the curious children of "Father Sky" and "Mother Earth."

Although it is customary in our culture to capitalize the word *God* when we are referring to our own Lord, we generally don't do the same for the Gods (gods) of others; in this book, we capitalize the term *God* when we are referring to all the deities. For the purpose of this book, we believe in all the Gods.

—*Steve Zeitlin*

In order to best reflect the culture in each story, I've based my artwork on actual designs, objects, or artifacts from that group of people. Rather than illustrate each story, I wanted to echo the visual imagination of that culture. The captions will tell you more about the sources I used.

—*Chris Raschka*

BETWEEN TWO PARENTS, EARTH AND SKY

In the cosmologies of the ancient Egyptians and the Maori people of New Zealand, two world parents, squeezed together in darkness, separate to create the earth and sky.

THE SKY-TOSSED UNIVERSE
OF THE MAORI PEOPLE

Imagine a God laid out against the sky with the sun resting on different parts of his body at different times of the day.

THE MAORI UNIVERSE was formed by the God of the Sky and Earth Mother who clung to each other with great passion until their children—crammed between them in the darkness—separated Earth and Sky, and created people from the bonds that held them together.

Centuries ago, according to Maori legend, a great fleet of long canoes sailed from a mythic homeland called Hawaiki (Tahiti). Straining at the oars, the Maori people rowed across great spans of ocean. They discovered the land we call New Zealand.

No part of New Zealand is farther than about eighty miles from the sea. Like the Maori canoes, the island is vulnerable to howling winds and wild waters. Many Maori stories pit wind against sea.

Based on ornamentation on a Maori Wakahuia feather box from the eighteenth or nineteenth century.

13

Yet, of all the Polynesian islands—Hawaii, Samoa, Tonga, Easter Island—New Zealand is the largest. Forests and plains, birds and other wildlife flourish on the landscape. In the myths of the Maori, the Gods of the Forest and the Gods of Planted Crops join the furious battles fought between wind and sea.

The British first arrived on the shores of New Zealand in December 1642, and the Maori fought a number of fierce wars against them. In 1845 the British sent the scholar-governor Sir George Grey to make peace in the islands. He believed that in the long run he couldn't govern unless he understood the language, manners, and customs of the Maori. This remarkable leader first set down Maori myths and beliefs in *Nga mahi a nga tupuna* (*The Deeds of the Ancestors*) in 1854.

THE CHILDREN OF RANGI AND PAPI

The Maori call their Sky God Rangi, and on bright days they observe the movement of the sun along his skyborne body. Each day, the sun rises to Rangi's left in the east and in the evening dips below the horizon on his right side in the west. During the year, the Maori observe how the sun gradually moves from Rangi's head down to his toes and then back again. When the sun is near Rangi's head, it is summer in New Zealand.

In the beginning, Rangi, the sky, lay upon Papi, the earth. Weeds covered the world. The sky was dark. The children lay between two Giants, unhappy in the never-ending darkness. Light had never broken upon these young creatures. Space did not exist; movement was difficult; and the children often had to find refuge in their mother's armpits. In the darkness, the child-Gods dreamed of the light. Each eon of darkness was called a Po, and the Gods chanted, "The Po, the Po, the Light, the Light, the seeking, the searching, in Chaos, in Chaos."

A fierce argument broke out among the children. Tu Matauenga, God of War, said, "Let us kill these parents of ours who have pressed our bodies together in darkness."

But Tane Mahuta, God of the Forests, answered, "No, let us separate them. Why not lift Sky high above the earth, so we can keep Earth close to us as our nursing mother? Let our father, Rangi, become as a stranger to us." The other offspring saw wisdom in this, except for Tawhiri Matea, God of Winds and Storms, who knew that he would be left with his father in the sky.

The young Gods decided to attempt the task of separation. First, Rongo Ma Tane, the God of Cultivated Food, positioned himself between the bosoms of his parents. With a hand on each chest, he tried to thrust them apart. He grunted and yelped but his parents would not budge. Then Tangaroa, God of the Sea, placed his hands on one, feet on the other, and tried to pry them apart. Still no movement. Next, Tu Matauenga leaped up. He bloodied Earth and Sky, hacking at the sinews that bound them together. The bright blood dried into (red) clay. Years later, human beings were made from that clay. But now, the two great and loving parents still clung to each other.

Only Tane Mahuta was left to attempt the task. First, he tried the techniques of his brothers. But even his great strength was not enough. So he placed his shoulders to the earth and feet to the sky, and, as a tree, began slowly to grow. Over thousands of years, Sky and Earth began to part. The sinews that bound them stretched and ripped apart as Tane Mahuta grew larger.

The parents cried out to the sons, "Why do you seek to separate us? How can you destroy the love we have for each other?" But the children of Rangi and Papi could now see the light that had been so long denied them. They could not live without it anymore.

They ran across Papi's body, admiring her figure shaped by mountains, hills, valleys, and wide rivers. They gazed with wonder at the light of the first dawn.

Yet Tawhiri Matea, God of Winds and Storms, was jealous of Tane Mahuta's achievement. He was afraid that because of his brother, the earth would become too beautiful, receive all the attention. He whirled to the top of the world where he consulted with Rangi and sheltered himself in the hollows of the boundless sky. From there, he brought horrible winds and storms to the corners of the earth. He begot an angry brood and sent them on a rampage: Fierce Squalls, Whirlwinds, Dense Clouds, Massive Clouds, Dark Clouds, Gloomy Thick Clouds, Fiery Clouds, Clouds Which Preceded Hurricanes, Clouds of Fiery Black, Clouds Reflecting Glowing Red Light,

Clouds Wildly Drifting from All Quarters and Wildly Bursting, Clouds of Thunderstorms, and Clouds Hurriedly Flying. In their wake followed the whirling God Tawhiri.

Behold, behold! The hurricanes rage. Great trees are snapped at the root. Branches are shattered and left for the insects.

Behold, behold! Tawhiri attacks the seas. Whirlpools threaten to pull all living things asunder. Waves break high as cliffs.

The Sea God, Tangaroa, hid deep in the ocean. His grandchildren panicked, wondering how to save themselves. For Tangaroa had given birth to Punga, and Punga had begotten Ika Tere, the Father of Fish, and Tu Te Wanawana, the Father of Reptiles. The grandchildren couldn't agree on where to flee. "Let us swim inland," some cried. "Let us swim to the sea," others exclaimed.

Finally, lizards and reptiles swam toward the land, and fish for the sea. Then the fish cried out, "Swim inland, and you will find yourself cooked in a bowl of soup." And the reptiles answered, "Swim to the sea, and they will fish you out and cook you over an open fire."

Tawhiri had now divided his brothers and set them to warring among themselves. Tangaroa grew furious that some of his offspring deserted the ocean, and, ever since, he has waged eternal war with his brother Rongo Ma Tane, God of Cultivated Food. Rongo Ma Tane supplies the Gods with canoes, spears, and fishhooks from his trees, nets from his plants. They seek to destroy the offspring of the Sea God,

Tangaroa. Tangaroa swallows them up in his water, turning over the canoes, flooding the land and the creatures that inhabit it, the many offspring of Rongo Ma Tane. Much of the land has been destroyed by Tangaroa's fury and is now submerged beneath the sea. To this day, the ocean laps and chews at the shoreline.

Papi and Rangi, Earth and Sky, remain far from each other's arms. Tears of mist and dew hover over Papi's woodlands. Rangi weeps tears of rain through the long nights.

In the old days, Heaven and Earth cried so hard for one another that fierce storms disturbed the sky. So their children conspired to turn Papi on her back. Now, the two great lovers no longer look so longingly into each other's eyes. The rain and storms no longer flood the lands.

Generations later, one of Rangi and Papi's great descendants, Maui—part man and part God—made a fishhook from the jawbone of an ancestor's skull. He cast the fishhook deep down into the ocean and snared a hefty piece of land. With all his might, he brought it to the surface where it became the Polynesian island country of New Zealand, the new Maori home.

THE SUN-CENTERED UNIVERSE OF THE ANCIENT EGYPTIANS

Imagine a boat that carries the sun across the sky each day.

IN THE EGYPTIAN UNIVERSE the sun God Re brings the sun out of the waters each morning on a boat called Millions of Years *and sails across the sky before sinking back into the sea at twilight.*

While the Maori of New Zealand spoke of the sky as a father and earth as a mother, the Egyptians pictured the universe the other way around—with an earth God, and a sky Goddess, Father Earth and Mother Sky.

Almost five thousand years ago, the people of ancient Egypt created one of the first human civilizations along a great desert on both sides of the Nile River. They relied on the river to water their crops. Each year, the Nile rose and covered their fields. In the springtime, as the waters subsided, the fertile land resurfaced for planting.

Based on an image of the Egyptian sky Goddess Nut, from about 1000 B.C.E.

21

The Egyptians believed that originally the God named Atum created the land and all of the universe as a hill rising up out of the river—just as their fields emerged from the Nile. God rose up out of the water and created the world because he needed a place to stand.

Atum was a sun God, "the one who created himself." The pharaohs of Egypt thought they were his incarnation here on Earth. Atum's blood flowed in their veins.

The myths of the Egyptians often depict the God Re, as Atum came to be called, as a man with the head of a hawk, tall as the heavens. "I am the creator of all things," he proclaimed. "I made earth and water. I created the sky to hold the souls of the Gods. I form the hours and the days and the time for the great festivals. I order the mysterious waters of the Nile to return each year. In the morning, I am known as Khepri, at midday as Re, and in the evening as Atum."

Eons later Re's grandchildren—Geb, the earth God, and Nut, the sky Goddess—lay together in a close and perfect embrace. Their father Shu the Uplifter decided to separate them so that they could fulfill their destiny. He placed his hands beneath Nut's belly and lifted her high above himself to form the arch of the heavens. He left his son Geb lying prone upon his back.

Nut arched over Geb, with her toes poised on the horizon in the east and her arms stretching to where her fingertips touch the horizon in the west. As the sun God Re set, Nut opened her mouth and swallowed him. During the night he was hidden from view as he passed through her body to be reborn at dawn from her loins in the east.

In some Egyptian myths, Re was pictured with a great eye in the center of his forehead that shone its light on the earth. In his battles with the wicked God Set, Re's eye was pulled from his face. Set placed it in the center of his own forehead. The God Osiris recovered the eye, but Set chopped off his head, eye and all. Osiris's son, Horus, healed Osiris with the milk of a gazelle and recovered the slippery eyeball. He restored the great eye of Re. Light again shone upon the earth.

EYE OF THE SUN

On a boat called *Millions of Years,* the God Re brought the sun out of the waters. He sailed across the air each day and sank into the waters in the evening.

Each night, Re's first nemesis, Apep, the great Serpent of Darkness, rose up against him. From the beginning of time, he tried to stop the sun from rising. The serpent hurled weapons of mist, rain, and darkness. He sent dark clouds to cover the sun.

Re's beautiful daughter, Isis, joined him upon the boat. They shot arrows that pierced the dark mists. And each day the sun broke through.

Re never forgot the danger and power of serpents like Apep. He gave orders to destroy all the snakes in the universe.

Many ages later, Re grew old and tired of lugging the sun across the sky. His bones grew thin, his muscles weary. But Re longed to keep working.

Re's wife, Nut, the lovely sky Goddess, took the form of a great cow. Each day, she carried him across the heavens. But she too grew tired and began to tremble under the weight. Her father, Shu, held up her belly so she could continue to carry the sun. Still, the God Re was exhausted. His body sagged and he began to drool.

His daughter, Isis, loved her father, but she wanted him to step down. She had secret motives for this: She wanted to take her place among the sky Gods, and she believed it was time for her son, Horus, to rule the universe. "My father, you have become an old man," she said. "The job of transporting the sun is too much for you."

He laughed and shook his head. "Never," he said.

Isis knew the secrets of Re's powers. He could be destroyed from a poison taken from the fluids of his own body. She swept up some of his saliva from his drool and molded a serpent by mixing his spittle with dirt.

Isis's serpent bit Re. The God began to tremble. The poison coursed through his veins as the river Nile spreads through the land of Egypt. With all of his powers, Re could not cure the wound, for the snake's poison was made from himself.

Gods gathered around him, consoling him and offering advice. From the edge of the crowd, Isis spoke. "Father," she asked in mock surprise, "what has happened? Has one of your own creatures bitten you? Has a creature you created lifted up its head against you? Father, I have studied the secret incantations with the Gods. I know the spells, and only I can cure you."

"Daughter," he said, "I have not been felled by fire, for I am burning hotter than fire. And I have not been hurt by water, because the pain is colder than water. I am shivering and shaking so that my very eye trembles and cannot see the sky."

Then Isis asked the question she knew he would never answer. "If you would like me to cure you, I must know your secret name."

Even in pain, with his face twisted, Re still winced at her request. But his faculties were clear, and he answered, as if to reveal his name, "I am the creator of all things. I made earth and water. I created the sky to hold the souls of the Gods. I form the hours and the days and the time for the great festivals. I order the mysterious waters of the Nile to return each year. In the morning, I am known as Khepri, at midday as Re, and in the evening as Atum."

Isis smiled knowingly. Her father was all these things. Those were among his many titles, but in his cunning, he had not revealed his secret name.

"You are wise," Isis laughed, "but you have not told me your secret name. Without it, I can devise no cure."

Re's pain grew more intense. He shivered and burned until he could hold back no longer. He called Isis into a secret chamber where no one could hear his words. Like merchants at a market, they began to bargain. But Re was too sick to bargain well. Isis told him the reason she needed the power of his name. "I want your two eyes—the sun and the moon—for my son Horus. It is time for him to rule over all creation."

Convulsed with pain, Re still did not say his name out loud. He whispered, "It is my will that Isis be given my secret name and that it leave my heart and enter hers." The name traveled soundlessly from the father's breast to the daughter's. The boat called *Millions of Years* lay empty. A thick darkness came over the land.

Then Isis kept her bargain and issued the incantation for pain. "Let Re live and let the poison die. Let the poison die and let Re live," she chanted. In the same breath, she willed, "O Eye of Re, go forth and shine from the mouth of Horus." The deed was done. Horus became king of all the Gods. Re retired, a graceful retirement indeed, for he was still honored by all as creator of all things. Isis appeared each year as Sirius, the brightest star in the heavens. She returned to the predawn sky each year when the Nile flooded its banks with life-giving waters.

SOMETHING OUT OF NOTHING

In the beginning, according to both the Hebrews and the Greeks, the universe lay in utter darkness and chaos and was created out of nothing.

THE BEAUTIFUL GODS OF THE ANCIENT GREEK UNIVERSE

Imagine a palace for the Gods atop the earth's highest mountain and a winged horse that returns home to a real barn.

THE ANCIENT GREEK UNIVERSE *was ruled by a beautiful race of Gods who lived in skyborne mountaintop kingdoms and underwater wonderlands.*

The ancient Greeks lived on a tough, hilly landscape bounded by the sea. Building homes on rocky terrain where only one-fifth of the land could grow crops, the Greeks depended heavily on rain. They believed the ruler of the universe was not, as the Egyptians had pictured, a sun God, but Zeus, who brought thunder and lightning when he hurled his mighty thunderbolt. Living near the Mediterranean and Aegean seas, the seafaring Greeks were traders and also worshiped Poseidon, God of the Sea.

Unlike the Egyptians who imagined their Gods with faces of jackals, hawks, and other animals, the ancient

Based on a painting of Zeus on a Greek vessel, or amphora.

Greeks saw the Gods in their own image. Bodies of the Gods mirrored not the beasts and birds, but beautiful women and men. In their myths, the Gods came from and moved about real places in ancient Greece.

The winged horse Pegasus returned each night to a stable in the city of Corinth. Heaven was a familiar place. Zeus, his wife, Hera, and many other Gods lived on Mount Olympus, the highest mountaintop in Greece. The Olympian Gods feasted on heavenly foods, ambrosia and nectar, and listened to the beautiful music of Apollo's stringed lyre.

Unlike the Egyptians, who believed that a God created the universe, the Greeks believed that the universe created the Gods. In the beginning, Chaos, the unformed darkness, separated itself into Night and Tartarus, the dark dwelling of the dead. In the words of the Greek playwright and poet Aristophanes, "black-winged night" laid a "windborne egg" in the dark bosom of Tartarus. The egg separated itself into Gaia (Mother Earth) and Uranus (Father Sky). Earth rose up, and the beautiful heavens formed to cover it on all sides and provide a home for the Gods.

The Greek myths, as we know them today, are the work not of priests but of poets. The most complete account of Greek beliefs on the creation of the world comes from the poet Hesiod, about whom little is known (scholars believe he lived sometime between 800 to 600 B.C.E.). He attributes his epic poem about the birth of the Gods, *Theogony,* to the Muses, the nine daughters of great Zeus, who brought the Greeks poetry and song. When the Muses sing for Zeus, Hesiod writes:

They thrill the great mind deep in Olympus,
Telling what is, what will be, and what has been . . .
And Zeus' mind in Olympus is thrilled by the song
Of the Olympian Muses, the Storm King's daughters. . . .

THE BIRTH OF ZEUS

Monstrous creatures sprang from the union of Mother Earth and Father Sky—three Giants, each with a hundred hands protruding from their shoulders and fifty heads growing on each of their stumpy necks; and three Cyclopes. The word *Cyclopes* means "wheel-eyed," and each had a single goggle eye in the middle of his forehead, big and round as a wheel.

Father Sky looked into his children's ugly eyes. Terror rose within him as he imagined that these ghastly creatures might one day become more powerful than he. He hurled the Hundred-Handed Giants and the hideous Cyclopes deep into the darkness of Tartarus, into the depths of the underworld.

Then Father Sky and Mother Earth gave birth to thirteen Titans, the first generation of Gods—Atlas, the most powerful; Prometheus, the most creative, who later molded the first humans from water and clay; Cronus, the youngest and most courageous, as mean-spirited as his father and known as the "arch deceiver."

In despair, Mother Earth came to Cronus and told him of his brothers, shamelessly imprisoned in Tartarus by their father. She gave Cronus her sickle. He sharpened it on the rocks of the Aegean Sea. One night, he approached his father as he lay sleeping and with one deft stroke, dismembered him and threw his parts into the sea.

Now Cronus ruled the universe. But he did not free his brothers, the Hundred-Handed Giants or the Cyclopes. "Let them stay right where they are," he said.

Time passed, and one night Rhea, Queen of the Universe, bowed before her husband's throne with a tiny bundle wrapped in her arms. "Cronus, my husband, Lord of the Universe," she said, "I have given birth to a beautiful baby girl. I present her to you and ask that you bless her with a name."

Children? Cronus thought, what do I want with children? I was my father's son, and look what I did to him! The wicked ruler of the universe, tall as a mountain, took the infant in his arms. "I will name you Demeter," he said scowling. Then he took the child, carried her to the palace window, and looked up toward the heavens. A wild and mad glint came into his eye. He stuffed Demeter into his mouth and swallowed her whole.

Rhea screamed in horror. She swore never to lie with her husband again. But she lived in his palace as a slave. Four more children were born to her, two daughters, Hera and Hestia, and two sons, Hades and Poseidon. Rhea tried in vain to reason with her wicked husband, but his madness only grew. As she presented him with each child, she watched in horror as his same twisted smile appeared. Then he stuffed each child into the opening in his face, which was as big as the mouth of a cave.

In despair, Rhea sought advice from Mother Earth, who instructed her wisely. "Come," she said, "I will show you a secret cave on the Isle of Crete. The next time a baby is born, hide the babe inside the cavern. Then wrap a rock in cloth as you would a baby. When he asks for the child, hand the stone to Cronus. I know my son. He will never know the difference."

Rhea followed her mother's advice. She gave birth to her son, the baby Zeus, and sheltered him in the secret cave. Cronus, hard-hearted and foolish, accepted the rock and swallowed it whole.

In the cave the infant Zeus fed on honey and on the milk of a goat named Amaltheia (later, in gratitude, Zeus placed her among the constellations in the sky). His cradle was safe in that Cretan cave. At its mouth, a group of young warriors clashed their swords and spears together and drowned out his infant cries. He could not be found in heaven nor on the earth nor in the sea.

When Zeus grew to manhood, he returned to his father's palace as a nobleman. In his plush chamber, his father, Cronus, offered Zeus a toast. But Zeus had laced his father's drink of nectar with poison. Cronus put the goblet to his lips and drank. His stomach erupted. He fell on the floor and clutched his sides. He vomited up the rock, followed by Poseidon and Hades. Then he choked up Hera, Demeter, and Hestia. But Cronus did not die.

Zeus told his father, who was still on the floor coughing,

"Now I, Zeus, the son you could not destroy, will rule the universe for all time."

But Cronus and his brothers, the Titans, resisted fiercely. Savage battles raged.

After ten bloody years, neither side could get the upper hand. Finally, Mother Earth called Zeus aside. "This fighting has gone on too long. There is something I must tell you. Like your father, your grandfather, Father Sky, worried that his sons would overthrow him. He gave birth to three Hundred-Handed Giants and three Cyclopes. He imprisoned them in the land of Tartarus beneath the earth. You must free them now and ask them to join in the battle."

Zeus descended into the earth and freed the first monstrous children of Mother Earth and Father Sky. He called the Cyclopes by their names. "Brontes, Steropes, and Arges, you are now free. Come with us to do battle against the evil Cronus who had the power to free you long ago." The Cyclopes agreed, and gave Zeus the gift of thunder and lightning.

In the final battle, Cronus led the Titans in a furious charge. The three Hundred-Handed Giants held hunks of cliffs in their rugged hands, and they hurled them to stop the Titans' advance. The three one-eyed Cyclopes held down the mighty Atlas. But Atlas broke free, tied them together, and rushed toward one of their large, round ugly eyes with a pointed stake. Through the hail of stones, Cronus twisted and mangled the arms of the Hundred-Handed Giants. The earth rumbled and crashed; the vast sky groaned; and Olympus shook under the immortals' onslaught.

Then Zeus hurled his mighty bolt, a whirlwind of flame.

The stake of Atlas shattered. Cronus broke loose from the Hundred-Handed Giants, and, with all the fury in his being, charged, his deadly arms extended.

Again, Zeus hurled the mighty thunderbolt.

Cronus sizzled and fell.

In defeat, Atlas, the strongest Titan, was forced to hold up the earth and sky. He became a pillar who bore that crushing weight on his shoulders for all eternity. The Cyclopes built Mount Olympus for the Gods.

Zeus and his brothers divided the universe among them. To determine who would rule what parcel of the universe, they cast lots. Zeus, the greatest of the Gods, proved luckiest. He became the Lord of the Sky, Rain God, and Cloud Gatherer. He was the God of the eagles and mountaintops, thunderstorms, oak trees, and all things tall. Zeus married his sister Hera, who became the Goddess of Marriage and Motherhood. Milk spurted from her breasts, creating the Milky Way. Poseidon with his trident inherited the sea. Hades became Lord of the Dead and the underworld.

Zeus placed the rock that Gaia fed to Cronus at the foot of Mount Parnassus to declare his conquest of the universe. Eons later, in 180 C.E., in the city of Delphi, a great traveler named Pausanias reported seeing it on display. The rock was said to be the "navel stone," marking the center point of the earth. Each day, the traveler wrote, the priests of Delphi anointed it with oil as part of their daily ritual.

THE ONE GOD OF THE HEBREW UNIVERSE

Imagine a God who created all of us in his (or her) own image.

THE HEBREW UNIVERSE was created by one God in six days.

The ancient Hebrews pictured the universe in a new way. Unlike the ancient Egyptians, they did not believe the Gods turned into the sun, moon, and stars after great battles with one another. Unlike the ancient Greeks, they did not believe in families of Gods who decided the fate of the world by waging war or drawing straws. There were no stories at all about this new Hebrew God. There were no myths about his childhood, how he came about, or how he was born.

This God did not create himself—he was just a given. How do we know what this God looks like? We are told that he created us in his own image; that is all. The Hebrew Bible, or Torah, concentrated on historical legends of the first generations of men and women: Adam

Rendering of an image from a sixth-century Jewish synagogue.   37 and Eve, Cain and Abel, Noah, and Job. There were no stories about God.

The Hebrews date their calendar from the creation of human beings, which their tradition considers to have been about 5,700 years ago. According to Jewish tradition, God dictated the Bible to Moses in about 1220 B.C.E., soon after the Jews fled the tyranny of the pharaohs, crossing the Red Sea into the desert. (Many scholars believe the Bible was actually written by a few generations of priestly scholars about six hundred years later.)

For Jews, and later for Christians and Muslims, the beautiful opening section of the first book of the Bible, known as Genesis, provides a vivid account of how the universe began and how the earth came to be. God creates the world by thinking and speaking it into existence. In the beginning was the word—when God says, "Let there be light," there is light.

As in many creation myths, light is created from the darkness. Time begins. The sky is separated from the earth, the land from the sea.

The story of Adam and Eve in the Garden of Eden explains how men and women were created and why all of us have to die.

GENESIS

In the beginning, God created the heaven and the earth. When he began, the earth was unformed, and the universe lay in total darkness. God's spirit hovered over the dark waters of nothingness. God said, "Let there be light." Suddenly, there was light.

God separated the light from the dark. He called the light Day and the dark Night. He caused them to follow each other. First there was evening, and then morning on the first day.

On the second day, God shaped the sky to curve over the earth. He created the dome of Heaven. Then he separated water from dry land.

On the third day, God said, "Let the earth bring forth grass, seeds, and fruit-bearing trees."

On the fourth day, God created a great light to rule the day, and a lesser light to rule the night. He made the sun and moon so that they would measure the seasons, the days, and the years.

On the fifth day, God created the birds and the fish.

On the sixth day, God created the cattle and all the other creatures of the earth. But he saw that something was missing. Then, from the dust of the earth, he created a man in his own image. He named the man Adam. While Adam slept, he pulled a rib from his side, and from it shaped the body of Eve.

He gave men and women power to rule over the beasts of the earth, the fish of the sea, and birds of the air. At the end of the sixth day, God looked at his creation and declared it was good.

On the seventh day, he rested. (To this day, the people of three religions set aside a day each week to commemorate God's day of rest—Muslims observe a weekly sabbath, a holy day of rest on Friday; Jews, on Saturday; and Christians, on Sunday.)

God entrusted Adam and Eve with the beautiful Garden of Eden, bordered by four great rivers, where marvelous fruits grew. He told them to make themselves at home. They could feast on any and all of the delectable fruits in the garden except one—the forbidden fruit that hung from the Tree of the Knowledge of Good and Evil.

But in the Garden lived a serpent, God's most evil and vile creation, jealous of God's power. He offered Eve a bite of the forbidden fruit. The fruit looked so tempting that she tasted it and offered some to Adam. Suddenly, Adam and Eve knew that they had wronged God. For the first time, they felt naked. They covered themselves with fig leaves.

God banished Adam and Eve from the Garden of Eden. From that day forth, he told them that they and all their children and their children's children would age and die. "I made you from the dust of the earth, and to dust you shall return." And so the first man and first woman betrayed God's trust and were banished from their garden paradise. But still God's love followed them through the gates and wherever they traveled forevermore.

CYCLES OF CREATION AND DESTRUCTION

The Hindus of India, like the ancient Norse of Scandinavia, believe the universe was created and destroyed, re-created and destroyed over vast periods of time.

THE ETERNALLY RECURRING UNIVERSE OF THE HINDUS

Imagine a God who can transform himself from a tortoise to a fish to a boar to a beautiful woman within a few moments.

THE HINDU UNIVERSE grew out of a beautiful lotus flower that sprouted from the God Vishnu's belly button.

Ancient India built great civilizations, only to have them destroyed and rebuilt. Agriculture in India dates back to 7000 B.C.E. Between 1500 and 1200 B.C.E., people in early Indian cities who spoke the Dravidian languages were overrun by the Indo-Europeans, who brought the language of Sanskrit and developed what was to become the Hindu religion. Then in 360 B.C.E., Alexander the Great conquered areas that are now in nearby Afghanistan and Pakistan. The Muslims invaded about 1000 C.E., and the British completed their conquest of India in the nineteenth century.

The myths of the Hindus spoke of great cycles of creation, destruction, and rebirth over even longer periods of time than these. In their ancient stories, the ages of man are composed of numerous long time periods called *maha yugas*. Each *maha yuga* lasted 12,000 divine years. Each divine year equaled 360 normal years, so the total number of years in a *maha yuga* was 4,320,000. Each cycle of creation and destruction lasted many *maha yugas*.

Hindu creation stories tell how the original force of the universe—called Brahma—separated itself into Brahma, Vishnu, and Shiva, the three great Lords whose tasks are to create, preserve, and destroy the universe again and again. Brahma creates; Vishnu sustains; and Shiva destroys. But Shiva's destruction is not always evil, for his destruction makes it possible for the universe to begin again.

The Hindu Gods have many incarnations. The ancient "Hymn to Vishnu" exclaims:

> *Fish! that didst outswim the flood;*
> *Tortoise! whereon earth hath stood;*
> *Boar! who with thy tusk held'st high*
> *The world, that mortals might not die;*
> *Lion! who hast giants torn;*
> *Dwarf! who laugh'd a king to scorn;*
> *Sole Subduer of the Dreaded!*
> *Slayer of the many-headed!*

Mighty Ploughman! Teacher tender!
Of thine own the sure Defender!
Under all thy ten disguises
Endless praise to thee arises.

In his most common incarnation, Vishnu has one thousand heads, two thousand eyes, two thousand legs, and two thousand arms. He is radiant, his clothing decorated with diamonds, rubies, and sapphires.

Depicted in luscious shades of red, Brahma has four faces and four arms, and controls a quarter of the universe with each face. He travels on a great swan, often carrying a spoon or a string of beads.

Once, after the universe was destroyed, a beautiful lotus flower sprang from Vishnu's belly button as he lay asleep across the great serpent Ananta as if on a silky bed. Encountering Vishnu in this position, Brahma realized that it was his destiny to be born from Vishnu's belly button. Vishnu invited Brahma to enter him. Inside, he saw all the ages of man. He then climbed through the belly button and the lotus flower.

A great egg formed around Brahma. Vishnu disappeared, and for eons Brahma slept inside the egg. Then crack—the egg began to hatch.

The crack and clamor of the hatching became the magical sounds of the universe. The place where the egg rested is Lake Samnihita in India. The egg hardened and became the earth. Brahma then created the sky, wind, rivers, oceans, streams, and mountains. He created women and men. He brought forth goats from his mouth, sheep from his chest, cows from his stomach. Demons curled out of his buttocks. For four *maha yugas*, the great God Vishnu preserved the universe. But when all of creation fell into its evil ways, the time came for Shiva the Destroyer, to fulfill his task.

Shiva, the great Lord of Death and Destruction, wears a tiger skin and is adorned with poisonous snakes. The river Ganga (Ganges) has its mouth in his lair. The crescent moon is in his hair. He wears a necklace of skulls around his neck, symbolizing the destruction and creation of mankind. His throat is stained blue from a deadly poison that would have destroyed the world forever but which he drank in order to save it. He carries a small drum that plays heavenly music. He dances all the time, a thousand heads and matching arms and legs shaking and bobbing. His partners are ghosts and ghouls known as *Ganas*. Millions of midday suns are in his body to set the earth and universe ablaze at the moment of total destruction.

RAHU'S RAGGED THROAT

With his fellow deities, Vishnu, the God with a thousand heads and two thousand eyes, conspired to create a dish called *soma,* the elixir of immortality. A single sip of that magical potion, and the Gods would live forever.

The elixir's preparation was a monumental task. For the recipe, the ocean itself had to be churned like a pail of milk until the potion emerged from it like butter. Not even the Gods could fulfill this task alone.

Vishnu enlisted the aid of the Demons, including the crafty Imp of Eclipses, the fiend Rahu. Together, they labored to use Mount Mandara, a massive peak in the Himalayas, as a churning stick. Vishnu transformed himself into a tortoise to steady the mountain. They twisted the great cliffs by pulling on the serpent Vasuki coiled around the rock. The cosmic sea thickened like cream around the mountain. Slowly, pieces of the universe came into being—the sun and moon, the Goddess of Wine, a magic tree, and the great elephant Airavata. Churning became most difficult, but finally a jug of *soma* congealed.

The Gods and Demons poured the elixir into bowls. The Gods drank. Then Vishnu watched as the Demons drew the bowls to their lips. As overseer of Creation, he could not allow these fiends to live forever. Before they swallowed, Vishnu transformed himself from a tortoise into a beautiful woman. Her deep gaze enchanted the Demons and put them to sleep.

Vishnu poured the Demons' elixir back into the jug and distributed it among the Gods.

Suddenly, the Demons awoke from the spell. Rahu grasped what had happened immediately. He saw that already most of the *soma* was gone. In an instant, he took on the appearance of a God, and with a swoop of his hand, swiped a swig of *soma.* Just then, he was spotted by newly created Sun and Moon. They whispered to Vishnu of the crime, and the God of Gods rushed to the scene. Vishnu gazed at Rahu's wily grin as the demon put the potion to his lips.

Just as the elixir of immortality began to slide slowly down Rahu's throat, Vishnu swung his sword and severed the demon's head. The potion never made it to the demon's belly but slipped out of his bloody severed gullet instead. With no claim on immortality, Rahu's body crumpled and fell to the earth.

But still, Rahu's head and jagged neck were bent upon revenge. He unleashed his fury on Sun and Moon, the pair who told Vishnu of his crime. To this day, he chases them around the sky. When he catches Sun or Moon and swallows them, all the world sees an eclipse. But the great orbs are never hidden from our gaze for long, for they slip right through Rahu's ragged throat and back to their rightful places in the sky.

THE BATTLEFIELD UNIVERSE OF THE NORSEMEN AND VIKINGS

Imagine riding the eight-legged horse Sleipnir over vast distances to the Land of the Frost Giants or to Hel, Land of the Dead.

THE NORSE UNIVERSE was defined by a World Tree with its top stretching almost to Asgard, stronghold of the Gods, and its three great roots leading to Midgard, Land of Humankind; Hel, the Land of the Dead; and Jotunheim, Land of the Frost Giants.

In medieval times the Vikings traveled on ships across the icy fjords, the narrow arms of sea surrounded by steep cliffs in Norway and Iceland. Raiding cities in Europe, they were known as sea robbers. But they were also daring explorers who reached as far as the shores of North America.

These Viking travelers were great poets and storytellers who recounted tales of the Norse Gods. On cold nights around a fire, as the wind blew across the frozen

Based on a Norse carving of Regin forging Sigurd's sword, from a church in Hylestad, Norway.

51

Scandinavian terrain, the Nordic story world took form—a place of darkness and terror, with tremendous barriers confronting travelers, human or divine, on journeys from one realm to another. In Norse myths and tales, great mountains and rushing rivers—like those of Norway and Iceland—often blocked the road. These ancient stories were first set down by a gifted Icelandic poet, historian, and politician named Snorri Sturluson around 1220 C.E. in a book called the *Prose Edda*.

In the beginning, a mighty tree stood in the center of a small bare island, surrounded by the sea. Animals dwelt in and under its twisted bark, and a great serpent curled round its roots. On its summit a cock perched, glittering like gold, and keeping watch. A mighty eagle nested high in its branches. When the eagle flapped its wings, great winds blew across the land.

The tree was threatened by the living creatures that scurried along its surface and made a home within its great rings. At its roots, the World Serpent joined a den of snakes that gnawed continually at its bark. The serpent waged war with the eagle, and a nimble squirrel ran up and down the tree carrying insults from one to the other. Goats and other horned creatures devoured the branches and tender shoots of the tree, leaping at it from every side. The World Tree—named Yggdrasil and sometimes called the Shelterer—suffered great anguish, but neither weapons nor fire could ever destroy it.

The tree had three mighty roots that stretched to the different realms of the kingdom—Midgard, the middle stronghold, home of humankind; Jotunheim, realm of the Frost Giants; and Hel, the Land of the Dead. The stronghold of the Gods, Asgard, lay above the tree.

The God Odin, attended by his two great ravens, Memory and Thought, rode far over land and sea, among all the kingdoms, astride the greatest of all steeds. On his eight-legged horse Sleipnir, he traveled the long and dangerous trails that led to Jotunheim or to Midgard. He entered the halls of kings, disguised as an old man in a broad-brimmed hat and cloak and sought adventure in the Land of the Frost Giants.

His son, the great red-bearded God Thor, made regular expeditions to Jotunheim to kill Trolls, wading through rivers and passing through mighty forests on the way. Thor possessed the hammer Mjollnir, which could slay Giants and shatter rocks; he owned a belt of power, which doubled his strength, and iron gloves to grasp the terrible hammer. In Asgard, Thor challenged Odin to games played on a silver board with glittering golden pieces. Odin's son Balder, said to be the fairest of all the Gods, watched his father play.

The mischievous Loki was the son of a Giant given to evil ways. Loki gave birth to the wolf Fenris, to the World Serpent, and to Hel, who ruled the Land of the Dead of the same name.

The Goddess Frigg was Mother Earth in disguise. She worked at the World Loom, and when her spindle spun, the celestial axis turned the sky to spin the thread of time.

The God Heimdall guarded the rainbow bridge Bifrost that began in Asgard and ended in Midgard. He blew a great horn to give warning to the Gods of attackers from the Land of the Dead. He needed less sleep than a bird; so keen were his ears that he could hear the wool growing on a sheep's back.

The road from Asgard to Hel took nine nights through deep, dark valleys, over rivers welling up from the lowest depths, across a second bridge, a bridge of fire that resounded under the marching feet of the dead. At the end stood the mighty gate of Hel.

The Gods traveled this bridge on their journeys, but it was doomed to be shattered in the battles that would rage on the earth's last day. As the ancient book of tales, the *Prose Edda,* foretells, "There will come a time, a barbarous age, an age of the sword, when brothers shall stain themselves with brothers' blood, when sons shall be the murderers of their fathers, and fathers of their sons, and no man shall spare his friend. Immediately shall succeed a desolate winter; the snow shall fall from the four corners of the world, the winds shall blow with fury, the whole earth shall be hard bound in ice. Three such winters shall pass away without being softened by one summer. Then shall the monsters break their chains and escape; the great serpent shall roll himself in the ocean, and with his motions the earth shall be over-flowed; the earth shall be shaken, the trees shall be torn up by the roots, the rocks shall be dashed against each other."

THE END OF THE WORLD

One night, Odin's son Balder, fairest of all divine beings, had a frightening dream about his own death. He told his father, who convened a council of the Gods. Fearing danger, the council sent the Goddess Frigg to extract an oath from every man, woman, and child, every plant, every thing made of metal, wood, and stone. All had to promise that they would do no harm to Balder.

Balder, told that the world's creatures had promised not to harm him, invited the Gods in the halls of Asgard to throw stones and darts at him. They all laughed as the missiles fell harmlessly from his body and bounced against the marble floors.

But the wicked Loki grew ever more angry. He took on the disguise of a woman and talked with Frigg. He learned that one little plant, the mistletoe, had not taken the oath. Frigg had thought it too young to threaten Balder. Filled with spite, Loki pulled up the little mistletoe and persuaded Hoder, the blind God, to hurl it at Balder, guiding his hand as he threw.

The mistletoe pierced Balder like a dart, and he fell dead to the earth.

Bitter tears fell from the eyes of the Gods, and Odin's were the most bitter of all. He asked for a warrior to ride to the kingdom of Hel and attempt to bring Balder back from the dead. Borrowing Odin's horse Sleipnir, the God Hermod rode down the dark road to that dim land, over the fiery bridge that spanned the Resounding River. A maiden guarding this bridge came out in wonder to see who approached with such noise and tumult. Balder, she said, had already passed that way, guarded by five troops of dead warriors. But he was not like the other dead men; he still had the rose-colored cheeks of the living.

At last Hermod reached the Hel gate, and Sleipnir leaped over it with ease. Balder was seated on the platform reserved for new arrivals. Hel was willing to release him on the condition that all things in the world, living or dead, would weep for him. But should any creature refuse to weep, she said, then Balder must stay with her and never return to Asgard. Hermod bid Balder farewell, and he and Sleipnir headed home.

At the request of the Gods, all things—men and beasts—did indeed weep for Balder. Even stones and metals became moist with tears. But as the messenger of the Gods traveled to the far reaches of the kingdom, he came upon a Giantess, alone in a cave. When he asked her to weep for Balder, she offered a horrible reply:

Alive or dead, the old man's son
has been no use to me.
Let Hel hold what she has!

The Giantess was none other than Loki himself, seeking in his malice to keep the fair Balder in Hel!

With Loki's wickedness unleashed in the universe, the ties of kinship and the rules of law collapsed. Evil ran rampant. The Giants crossed the sea in a boat made of dead men's finger-nails, with Loki as the steersman. They crossed the bridge of fire, tearing it asunder with their weight. The vicious wolf Fenris held the sun and moon and the space between earth and heaven between his deadly jaws. The World Serpent emerged from the deep, foam spewing from the corners of his mouth.

When the fiends neared the Rainbow Bridge, the sound of Heimdall's horn and the crowing of the cock on the World Tree heralded the approach of the enemy. When the signal came, Odin led his army out onto the field where the last battle was destined to be fought. Fire flashed from the eyes and nostrils of the wolf Fenris as he devoured the sun. The mighty serpent vomited great torrents of venom upon the waters. The stars flew from their places, and the heavens cracked open.

Odin's sharp blade tore into Fenris; his horse Sleipnir, up on his hind legs, clawed at the wolf. Valiantly they strug-gled, but the savage Fenris devoured them both. Odin's young son Vidar avenged his father, tearing the monster's jaws apart.

Wearing his belt of power, Thor swung the hammer Mjollnir, flattening the great serpent. Dying, the serpent bit him, and the mighty Thor crumpled, slowly twisted to the ground, and died from the poison. Heimdall and Loki slew each other. The sky fell, and the stars vanished. Fire and smoke rose high, and the rising sea engulfed the world.

But this was not the end, for the World Tree survived untouched. During the terrible winter struggle, the sons of the Gods, along with a single man and woman, sheltered within its bark. When the devastating battles ended, they came out into the bright light to begin their lives anew. Once more an eagle was seen in the sky, and a new sun moved across the heavens. As they rested on the fresh grass of the cleansed world, the young Gods found the golden playing pieces for the games that Odin and Thor once enjoyed in Asgard.

AT THE CENTER OF THE UNIVERSE

*The early scientists of Europe believed the earth
was at the center of the universe.*

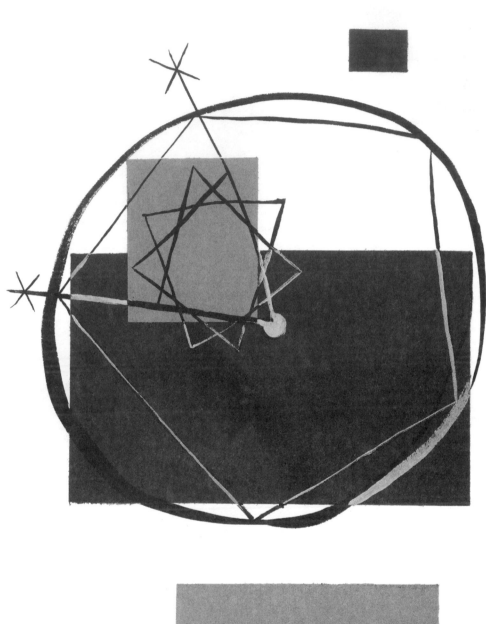

THE EARTH-CENTERED UNIVERSE OF EARLY WESTERN SCIENTISTS

Imagine the task faced by scientists in the days before telescopes when they had to figure out the cosmos with the naked eye.

THE UNIVERSE OF EARLY WESTERN SCIENCE *revolved around the earth.*

In the sixth century B.C.E., Thales of Miletus, often considered the first Western scientist, traveled from his home in Asia Minor to Egypt where he became familiar with Egyptian mythology. Each year, the Egyptians (as we have seen) watched the land reemerge from the Nile for planting in the spring and attributed this event to the God Atum. Thales believed that the earth arose from the waters in the same way, but he left Atum out. He believed Gods and Goddesses were not necessary to explain the forces of nature.

Thales' good friend and associate Anaximander of Miletus was the first Greek to make a map of the known

Rendering of "Proposito VI" (Proposition VI) in *Harmonices mundi libri V,* a book by the scientist Johannes Kepler.

61

world and create a celestial globe, showing the patterns of the constellations in the sky. Anaximander believed the sun, moon, and the stars were great balls of fire. They appeared as dots and circles in the sky not because they were so far away, but because they were seen through holes in the moving dome of the heavens.

Seven centuries later, a scientist named Claudius Ptolemaeus (Ptolemy, ca. 127–151 C.E.) worked in the great library at Alexandria in Egypt. In that ancient library all the books were handwritten on parchment scrolls, and many existed in a single copy. At this famed center of learning, Ptolemy proposed that the sun and the planets revolved around the earth.

Ptolemy's theory could explain why it was light and dark about half the time. His ideas, however, didn't mesh with some of most accurate observations of his day. For example, observers had already noted that the planets sometimes appear to be moving backward (today this phenomenon is called retrograde motion).

The actual reason for this "backward movement" is that some of the planets are farther away from the sun than we are. They revolve around the sun on an outside track, and the earth passes them in its orbit, so they appear to be moving backward. To explain this in a way that was consistent with his theory that the sun revolved around the earth, Ptolemy imagined that the sun and the planets moved in perfect circles around a point in space that was, in turn, revolving around the earth.

He also imagined the sun and planets were each attached to a transparent sphere made of crystal. As the planets revolved around the earth, their invisible sphere turned, although it looked to us as if only the planets were moving. The sun had a sphere of its own, and all of the stars were connected to their own sphere. There was one for the moon, and for the planets known in those days—Mercury, Venus, Mars, Jupiter, and Saturn. There was a separate sphere for Heaven. (This notion was disproved by astronomer Tycho Brahe in the sixteenth century, when he noticed that comets soared by the planets without ever shattering those crystal spheres!)

Many scientists of Ptolemy's day believed these heavenly bodies created a wondrous sound as they turned, "the music of the spheres." We mortals are not aware of this beautiful music made by the planets because we've been hearing it since we were born. We've become so used to the sounds that we've tuned them out.

In the centuries following Ptolemy, the Christian church played a powerful role in European people's lives. Many of the thinkers about the cosmos of that time were called "natural philosophers," and they tried to reconcile what was known of the stars and planets with the account of Creation in the Bible. Some argued that the universe operated by natural causes, but they imagined a group of Angels providing the original force that moved the planets and stars. Drawings of the universe actually showed Angels turning cranks to make the sun and planets revolve around the earth.

Thirteen centuries passed between Ptolemy and a Polish Catholic cleric named Nicolaus Copernicus, who put forth a radically different theory of the universe. Drawing on more accurate observations, he recognized that Ptolemy's theory did not fully explain the way the planets appeared to move backward. It was more accurate to assume that the sun and the planets did not revolve around the earth but that the earth and planets turned around the sun. He proposed a *heliocentric* (sun-centered) rather than a *geocentric* (earth-centered) universe. Just as a child needs to learn that he or she is not the center of the universe, humanity needed to learn that our planet was not the center point of the cosmos, the heart of everything.

Born in 1571, Johannes Kepler, another of the great astronomers, embraced the Copernican universe. Employing astronomical calculations, Kepler came up with a basic, remarkable observation that revolutionized the way we look at the universe. Since the time of the Greeks, scientists believed that all orbits had to be perfectly circular. They invented orbits within orbits to explain the movement of the planets and still maintain their belief in perfectly circular paths. Kepler realized that these planetary paths were not perfect circles, but ovals, or *ellipses.* Because of his bold stroke of genius, the universe became easier to chart and understand.

For Kepler, the universe was still straightforward enough to imagine as a simple machine. He compared it to a grand clock. He suggested that one force, magnetism, served as the weight which would make the celestial clock go round.

In Kepler's time, and for sometime afterward, scientists were fond of constructing models of the universe as clocklike machines. One version of the later models was called an *orrery*—in which the turning of a handle causes an ingenious system of gears to make the earth and the planets revolve around the sun, and the moon revolve around the earth.

Then, in 1609, a great scientist named Galileo heard about a magnifying device that was being sold by a Dutch gentleman who made glasses partly to amuse children. He purchased the gadget and began perfecting it as a telescope to look at the stars and the sky.

When Galileo pointed it toward the heavens, he could see countless stars that he had never seen before. He could see craters on the moon and sunspots. He observed that the Milky Way was made up of individual stars that could not be seen with the naked eye.

Many astronomers after him, Edmund Halley (1656–1742), William Herschel (1738–1822), and, in our time, Edwin Hubble (1889–1953)—and the telescope named after him—have improved the way we look at the endless expanse of the universe. But today's scientists are standing on the shoulders of great thinkers such as Thales and Ptolemy as they look farther and more accurately into space. In a sense, they are poking their heads through a hole in the sky to see where we are in the cosmos.

MIRRORING THE COSMOS

The cosmos of the Incas, the Jains, the Desana Indians, and the Haitians are mirror images of life on the earth.

THE MILKY WAY MIRRORED IN THE HIGHWAYS OF THE INCAS

Imagine a city or a kingdom laid out in a way that mirrors the positions and the movements of the sun, moon, and stars.

THE INCA UNIVERSE is reflected in the placement and structure of its temples and highways.

Have you ever looked up at the sky at night and seen the creamy stream of stars known as the Milky Way? These stars are the spiral galaxy, the collection of stars, gas, and dust that includes our own solar system and its planets. Our portion of the universe, according to today's scientists, is shaped less like a ball than a saucer. For that reason, it appears to us as a band across the sky.

Today, our calendars are set according to the yearly journey of the earth around the sun. But the Incas and their predecessors along the Andes mountain chain in South America defined their seasons according to the

Milky Way. They called the star stream Mayu, the "Celestial River." Some scholars believe they laid out their roadways based on the path of the Milky Way.

As the earth revolves around the sun, one hemisphere tilts toward our fiery star for half the year and away from it the other half—that is what makes the seasons change. For this reason, we see the Milky Way from a different perspective in summer and in winter. Since the position of the earth changes each day as we revolve around the sun, the Milky Way appears to take a slightly different place in the sky each night. As the Incas looked up into the night sky, they saw the Milky Way pursue a wobbly course, slanting left to right half the year and right to left the other half.

The Incas believed that the two opposing arcs formed by the Milky Way during its highest point in summer and winter intersected at a set point. They thought that the two intersecting sky streaks divided the world into four quarters. The sprawling empire of the Incas was consequently named Tahuantinsuyo, "Land of the Four Quarters."

In the fifteenth century, the Incas conquered the peoples of the rugged Andes mountain chain. To the west their kingdom reached the dry Atacama Desert; to the east it stretched to the edges of the Amazon Rainforest. The Incas ruled what was to become northern Chile, upland Argentina, Bolivia, Peru, Ecuador, and the south of Colombia.

In their capital of Cuzco, the Incas built two grand highways intersecting at their magnificent central plaza, mirroring the intersection of the summer and winter travels of the Milky Way. The two highways traveled outward throughout their kingdom of Tahuantinsuyo. At the intersection of the highways in the center of town stood the *capac usnu,* a vertical pillar with a sculpted seat where the emperor, "the son of the sun," ran affairs on the earth. From his throne at the center point of the universe, he reviewed processions at the intersection of the highways as he toasted the Gods.

THE ROD OF GOLD

The nighttime stars of the Milky Way shaped the way the Incas laid out their kingdom. But they also worshiped the daytime sun. In the beginning, the sun God Viracocha rose from the waters of Lake Titicaca on the border of what is now Bolivia and Peru. He created humans out of clay. But, alas, his new creations did not possess the basic skills for survival. They could not master weaving, and they knew nothing about how to farm. Viracocha felt sorry for them.

He approached his son and daughter, the Inca (the name for both the people and their King) and his Koya (Queen), born of the moon Goddess. He told them of the mission he had set for them—to instruct the hapless people below on planting, house building, and how to weave clothes.

Before his children began their task, he presented them with a golden rod, half the length of a man's arm, and two fingers thick. Wherever they stopped to eat or sleep, they were to press the rod against the ground. When they found a place where the rod entered the ground and disappeared with a single stroke, they were to found a great city, capital of all Creation.

"You must rule the people wisely and justly. Have mercy and tenderness. Treat them as a father would treat his children, just as I would, for it is I who care for the world and bring it warmth and light. I name you the rulers over all those people whom you will lift up with your good instruction, your just laws, and skillful governance."

Then the two children, like their father, rose up from Lake Titicaca and began traveling northward. After many stops, the Inca and his Koya entered the Valley of Cuzco. When they stopped to rest, they placed the tip of the rod against the dirt. It disappeared with a single stroke. They founded the city of Cuzco and built the temple of the sun on the very spot where the rod entered the soil.

THE COSMOS AS A WOMAN IN THE MYTHOLOGY OF THE JAINS

Imagine a universe that took the shape of a human being.

THE UNIVERSE OF THE ANCIENT JAINS took the form of a colossal person.

Unlike the Egyptians, the Greeks, the Hindus, and the Hebrews, the Jains, a sect in central and western India, did not believe their universe was ever created—it was always there. It had no beginning or ending in time. In Jain art from about the sixteenth century onward, the cosmos was depicted as *lokapurusha*, a giant woman or man. The Jain unit of measurement was the "rope," or *rajju*, the distance traveled by a God flying for six months at a speed of ten million miles per second. The cosmic Giant of the Jains measured fourteen ropes from head to foot.

Mount Meru, the Golden Mountain, was in the navel of a cosmic Goddess who contained the universe within her. Around the mountain was the Circle of the Lotus, where human beings lived. Moving outward was the Ocean of the Lotus, the Circle of Milk and the Ocean of Milk, the Circle of Butter and the Ocean of Butter, the Circle of Sugarcane and the Ocean of Sugarcane. Then, after many more circles, the Land of the Joy of Being Oneself, and, beyond that, the Ocean of the Joy of Being Oneself.

Beneath all the circles, seven hells—each one darker and more dismal than the other—filled the Goddess's pelvis, legs, and feet. The creatures of these seven hells suffered endlessly the demonic tortures of their jailers.

Above the navel, fourteen celestial stories formed the Goddess's chest, shoulders, neck, and head. A spot above the head was the place of perfection in the universe called Slightly Tilted. Through lifelong prayer and the practice of a physical religious exercise called yoga, the soul of the righteous would ascend and be released through that perfect spot in the Goddess's head.

THE UNIVERSE AS A BRAIN
IN THE DESANA INDIAN
COSMOS

---

*Imagine that the dark dome of the sky resembles
the brain inside our heads.*

*IN THE UNIVERSE OF THE DESANA INDIANS the night sky is a
cosmic Brain, reflecting each individual's consciousness.*

When Michelangelo painted the ceiling of the Sistine
Chapel, he portrayed God as a powerful old man with a
beard. Human beings have often found ways to project
themselves onto the universe. While the Jains of India
depict the cosmos as a colossal person, the Desana of the
Amazon imagine it as a giant brain.

At the beginning of time, the Desana believe, their
ancestors sailed in canoes shaped like huge serpents
along the Vaupés River to their present home in the
Amazon Rainforest of Colombia. The Desana Indians
of the northwest Amazon are a tiny tribe of about six
hundred people. As hunters who often use clubs to kill
their prey, they are familiar with the brains of monkeys

and other animals. Brains play a large part in how they understand the world around them.

The Desana see the brain as divided into left and right hemispheres, or halves. They believe ideas, information, and spiritual enlightenment move between the two sides. The divide between the two hemispheres is imagined as two entwined snakes, one a dark-colored female anaconda, the other a brightly colored male rainbow boa. The right side of the brain is female, the left male. The female side contains all practical information about plants and animals, all of the Desana customs and rituals. The female side also puts into practice the theoretical ideas that exist on the male side of the brain.

Like a brain, the Desana sky is divided in half. The Milky Way, a group of stars that comprises our own galaxy and appears as a white band in the sky, divides the two halves. To the Desana, the Milky Way consists of the same two entwined serpents that cleave the human brain—one an anaconda, the other a rainbow boa. The male boa is associated with land and light and color. The female anaconda is associated with water and darkness. As the serpents spiral around each other, they mark out the cycles of night and day.

Contemporary scientists have discovered that the human brain really is divided in half. Like the Desana, they suggest that each side provides a different kind of thinking, although they don't divide the types of thought in the same way. The two halves of the brain are separated by a deep groove. At the base of the groove is a thick bundle of nerve fibers called the corpus callosum, which provides the communication link between the two halves.

The Desana believe that their own brains are in harmony with the sky Brain. The harmony between brain and sky makes all thought possible.

THE TWIN WORLDS OF THE HAITIAN UNIVERSE

Imagine that we all have a twin Spirit wandering around somewhere in a parallel universe.

THE HAITIAN UNIVERSE includes a mirror image of our own world where the twin Soul of each of us resides.

On the Caribbean island of Haiti, Vodou practitioners don't worship a single God; they serve many Spirits— and the Spirits are beautiful, sometimes frightful, and quite human. The Vodou spirits are not unlike the Greek Gods and Goddesses of Love and War who inter vene in everyday human affairs. But unlike the Greek Gods whom we know about through the work of poets, the Gods of Vodou are part of the day-to-day religion of many Haitian people. These Haitians enact their cosmology, their picture of the universe, with every ritual ceremony.

The Haitian Mount Olympus is not on a mountaintop but below the earth. Many Haitians believe in the

Rendering of a Haitian *vévé*, a design drawn on the ground to symbolize the entry into the underworld.

world of *Les Invisibles,* "the Invisibles"—a world of Gods and Goddesses called *Loas* (or *Lwas*) who exist in the waters below the earth. The world of *Les Invisibles* is a mirror image of the everyday world. Vodou priestesses often begin a religious ceremony by walking backward toward the altar, illustrating how the world of the Gods is a reversed mirror image of the human world.

To Vodou believers the universe is a circle, and the lands of the living and the dead are separated by a horizontal line. Here on the earth, we dwell on the upper sphere. The dead dwell under the water. Journeying through the sky, the sun visits the dead and the living at opposite times. Noon for the living is exactly midnight for the Spirits of the dead.

Followers of Vodou believe that our world and the world of the Gods are joined at certain points they call the crossroads, presided over by the God Legba. At the crossroads, a great tree often penetrates the earth, creating a passageway from our world to the land of *Les Invisibles.* At every Vodou ceremony in Haiti, and in cities such as New York where Haitians have immigrated, the great tree is symbolized by a pole in the center of the prayer space, where the rituals take place.

On the floor around the center pole, the Vodou priestesses, called *manbos,* draw pictures made up of simple shapes called *vévés.* To do this, they hold a small amount of flour between thumb and forefinger and let it sift to the ground. These *vévés* serve as doorways to the underworld.

Summoned by the pounding of the drum, the *Loas* appear in this world by taking possession of a living person. A dancer during the ritual goes into a trance and is taken over by the God. The signs are clear—the head shakes; the legs stiffen; and the body moves violently as if being pushed by an external force. He or she speaks in the God's voice, and "becomes" one of the Gods—Erzili, Ghede, Legba, or others. A person who has been possessed is said to have been "mounted" by a Divine Horseman, or *Loa*. When the Gods depart, the man or woman they are "riding" often collapses from exhaustion and cannot remember what happened. While possessed, they may eat the many offerings of chicken or eggs or sweets to the God, but upon awakening, remain hungry.

For the Haitians, every man and woman has a Spirit, or Soul, in the land of the Gods. When a believer dies, family and friends worship the Spirit of the dead person, believing that his or her twin Spirit continues to exist in the underworld. They call that Spirit back during religious ceremonies, and even put out a *govi,* a clay jar to hold the Soul of the dead. Over time, the Soul of the person who dies becomes an ancestor, and over the generations the Souls merge back into one of the *Loas.* If the one who died was powerful and strong, that Soul might become associated with the God of War, Ogou; if they were gentle and loving, with the Goddess of Love, Erzili.

The Vodou God Ghede, the Lord of the Dead, who appears at many Vodou ceremonies, resides in graveyards and loves to misbehave. He is considered to be the corpse of the first man.

A UNIVERSE OF ANIMALS AND PLANTS

In the cosmologies of the Fon of Africa and of the Iroquois and Chumash North American Indian tribes, a turtle shell, a coyote, or a calabash are the building blocks for the universe.

THE TURTLE-SHELL WORLD
OF THE IROQUOIS

Imagine our planet as a living organism like an animal or a plant.

THE IROQUOIS UNIVERSE *was created on a turtle's broad back.*

At the Turtle Museum in upstate New York, a large turtle shell hangs on the wall. The thirteen scales on the shell are numbered, marking out the thirteen months of the Iroquois calendar. Many Native American tribes measured time according to the cycles of the moon. Each year had thirteen lunar months. As Abenaki Indian writer Joseph Bruchac put it, beautifully, there are "thirteen moons on turtle's back."

In the myths of many North American Indian tribes, an "Earth Diver" assisted in the creation of the world. In these stories, small animals attempted to dive deep into the sea to bring up the mud necessary to create the earth.

Taken from the design on a Chippewa drum.

One after another failed. Most often a muskrat, a beaver, or a crawfish was the creature who succeeded, returning to the surface half dead with some sand or dirt in his claws. That bit of earth became the world.

For Indians east of the Mississippi River, particularly among the "Six Nations" of the Iroquoian Confederacy (Mohawk, Onondaga, Oneida, Cayuga, Tuscarora, and Seneca tribes), the theme of the Earth Diver is coupled with stories about the great Earth Turtle. The fabled Turtle carries the moon calendar on his shell, and the world on his broad back.

ON A TURTLE'S BACK

In the beginning our world, the lower world, curled in a cocoon of darkness. But far beyond the dome we call the sky was a much older world known as the Blue. Creatures that looked a lot like humans inhabited this Up-Above-World. A tree covered with white blossoms stood at the center. The lovely aroma of sacred tobacco wafted upward from its roots. When the tree was in bloom, the people could see by its light. When the blossoms fell from its branches, the Blue was covered in darkness.

The Up-Above-World was ruled by a Great Chief who fell in love with a beautiful woman. She was called Sky Woman, and he took her for his wife. They ate the marriage bread together, and he brought her to his lodge by the great tree. To his dismay, he discovered that she was already pregnant, ready to give birth to a child.

"Who is the father of this child?" he asked her.

"The West Wind," she replied.

The Great Chief grew jealous and angry. That night he dreamed that the tree with white blossoms should be pulled up by its roots. The next day he told his people of his dream. "A circle must be dug around the great tree," he told them. His men cut around the roots, and the tree fell through the bottom of the Blue.

The tree with blossoms was gone, and no new light came to take its place. The aroma of sacred tobacco no longer filled the air. The Chief was sad and angry. He summoned Sky Woman.

"Woman," he said, "seat yourself on the edge of the hole, and see what is down there." As she sat looking into the opening, the angry Chieftain pushed the woman with his foot. She dropped down through the hole.

Sky Woman fell through great expanses of darkness before she entered the bright light of our sky. She plummeted through the air. Looking down, she could see only a large body of water.

The creatures of the deep looked up when she struck the surface.

"Look," said one of the monsters, "a creature is falling through the waters."

As she twisted and turned in her descent, the great monsters of the deep became alarmed, and summoned a gathering of underworld creatures. They pondered ways to keep her from falling through the underworld. One creature said, "We cannot hold her. She is too heavy."

"She is sinking too fast," another said.

As Sky Woman tumbled, her arms and feet flailing around her in the water, a slow-moving creature approached the gathering. It was a large tortoise. "I am the only creature steady enough to bear her weight," he said. "But I must have my shell softened with mud and earth from the deep."

The waterfowl offered to help. Duck and Gull dived down as deep as they could, but they could not reach the bottom. Finally, Crawfish attempted the task. The pressure of the deep almost tore him apart. But he reached down with his claw and pulled up some clumps of mud. He lurched upward through the water until he found Turtle. Almost dead, he placed the mud on Turtle's back. Duck and Gull smoothed it over.

Turtle watched the woman plummeting through the waters. He positioned himself upon the spot toward which she headed. Sky Woman, frightened, landed suddenly on Turtle's broad back. She breathed a sigh of relief.

When she was fully rested, Sky Woman walked in a counterclockwise circle upon Turtle's back. Turtle's shell widened to become an island of earth. Seeds sprouted from the mud on her back. The woman walked in wider circles. Turtle expanded. Bushes and trees grew upon her, and she grew as wide as the world, surrounded by water.

In this new Turtle World, Sky Woman gave birth to the

forces of good and evil. Her first son was born handsome and kind. But the second son forced himself out from under her arm and destroyed his mother with his birth. He was covered with boils and warts.

Her first child had a good disposition and was named Got-ti-gah-rah-quast, the Good Mind. Her second was evil and was named Got-ti-gah-rak-senh, the Twisted Mind. Good Mind was not content in the darkness. He was determined to create a great light in the dark world. Twisted Mind was desirous that the world should remain in darkness. Good Mind took his mother's head and placed it in the sky as the sun. He took her body and created a second light, the moon. The two brothers battled for many years, until Good Mind defeated his brother. The Good Mind visited the people one last time and then retired from the earth.

Today, in their circle dances, American Indians up and down the East Coast turn counterclockwise. Some say it is to honor Sky Woman and the direction she walked on Turtle's back.

THE CALABASH WORLD OF THE FON

Imagine a universe created not by world parents such as Father Sky and Mother Earth but by a God/Goddess who possessed both sexes in a single being.

IN THE FON UNIVERSE *the earth is like a great calabash, its weight supported by a coiled serpent resting in a deep blue sea.*

In Benin, home of the Fon people in west Africa, different kinds of calabashes grow on trees and vines. Many dishes, bowls, and drinking vessels are fashioned from the hard, large, round calabash fruit. Generations of great storytellers and proverb tellers have told their tales in the Fon language, accompanying themselves and one another on the *kora,* a large stringed instrument made from the calabash.

The Fon did not believe that the universe was comprised of Father Sky and Mother Earth. They believed in

Mawu-Lisa who was both God and Goddess, man and woman. The God/Goddess had two faces. Lisa's face had the eyes of the moon, Mawu's of the sun. Mawu-Lisa traveled with a great serpent, Aido-Hwedo, who accompanied the deity as he/she created the world in the shape of a great calabash. Where the serpent curled and wound, there were high places and low places, mountains and valleys.

When the world was finished, Mawu-Lisa looked about at the mountains, the trees, and the animals. Mawu-Lisa said, "The earth has too much weight," and asked Aido-Hwedo to coil himself around the bottom of the earth. "You shall be a carrying pad beneath the earth," he was ordered.

As both man and woman, Mawu-Lisa became pregnant. Two of the children Sogbo and Sagbata, were sent out into the sky. "You must be together like a closed calabash," Mawu-Lisa told them. "The world must exist inside you. Sagbata, you will travel to the earth. You must be as the lower part of the calabash. Sogbo, you will remain in the sky. You must be the upper part." Many stories are told about Sogbo, Sagbata, and their quarrels.

The earth-calabash continues to rest comfortably on the curled serpent, Aido-Hwedo. But one day, it is said, the serpent will swallow its tail, and all the earth will topple into the sea.

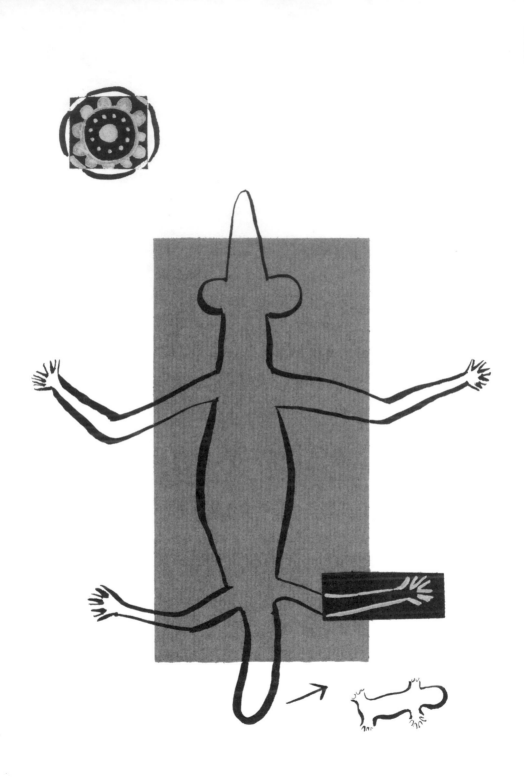

THE CHUMASH SKY COYOTE AND HIS YEARLY BATTLE WITH THE SUN

Imagine that the earth's first animals and human beings went on to become the moon and the stars.

IN THE CHUMASH UNIVERSE the Sun and the North Star play a game of chance to decide the fate of the earth's harvest.

Every year, the Chumash Indians of coastal California had to worry about whether their annual harvest would bring sufficient food to last the winter. When supplies dwindled, many of them starved. Feeding the tribe was difficult. Life and death hung in the balance.

The Chumash believed that in the early days of the world, animals could talk. They were known as First People. When death arrived on the earth, First People escaped into the sky to become the sun, the moon, and stars. The Chumash, who came later, no longer lived forever and had to take their chances here on the earth.

Rendering of a pictograph from the Tule River Reservation.

Among the Chumash, as in many Native American tribes, the foxlike coyote was a clever, tricky, wily creature—a trickster—in myths and stories. The Chumash told of a skyborne version of Coyote. They associated him with the North Star.

The Chumash thought of the sun and stars as animals and people. As the Chumash storyteller María Solarez put it, "Each one of those beings has a task to perform. Sun lights the day, Morning Star the dawn, and Moon the night. Moon is a single woman. She has a house near that of the Sun. She and the Sun and the others never get older. Snilemun (the Sky Coyote) was like God to the old people. Sun is our uncle, but Sky Coyote is our father—that is why he works for us, giving us food and sparing our lives."

The Chumash imagined the sun as an old man with a fire brand in his hand. According to María Solarez, both Sun and Evening Star eat people. The place where Evening Star lives is surrounded by hills and hills of bleached white bones of the people he has eaten.

Much of what we know about the Chumash comes from anthropologist John Peabody Harrington (1884–1961), who collected stories and other information about the Chumash for more than forty years, beginning in 1914. This wonderful story below was told to him by María Solarez from the Santa Ynez Valley, who died in 1922.

THE SKY PEOPLE

There is a place in the world above where Sun and Evening Star play a game of *peon* against the Coyote of the Sky and Morning Star. Sun and Evening Star are partners in the *peon* game. They have a lot in common—they both eat people. Both their team and Coyote's team try to guess in which hand a member of the other team is hiding a stick. The Moon keeps the score, awarding a point to the winner of each round. Once all the sticks have been played, the Moon declares the winner.

On Christmas Eve the Moon decides which side has won the game. When the Coyote's side comes out ahead, there is a rainy year. Sun places all kinds of harvest products—acorns, deer, ducks, and geese into a pile. Sky Coyote does not have the patience to wait until they are distributed. So he flings open the door so that everything falls down into this world.

We humans are involved in this game. When Sky Coyote's team wins, we gather up the food. When Sun's team wins he receives his pay in human lives. He and Sky Coyote then have a dispute, for the Sky Coyote, when he loses, wants to pay his debt with old people. But once in a while Sun wins the argument, and a young person may be picked out to die.

THE COSMIC EGG

The ancient Chinese and contemporary scientists both suggest that the universe burst forth from a single concentrated point of matter and energy.

Hatching the Ancient Chinese Universe

Imagine a universe created by the act of separating opposites such as hot and cold, darkness and light.

THE ANCIENT CHINESE UNIVERSE *was made from the body of the first man, the Giant P'an Ku.*

In the beginning was an egg. Within, cold and hot, male and female, wet and dry, earth and sky, dark and light— all the opposites needed to create the universe—blended and mixed. Inside the egg, P'an Ku, the first man, separated these pairs of opposites, called the yin and yang, just as the yolk is separated from the white inside a chicken's egg. Then P'an Ku burst forth from the egg. The universe was created.

As P'an Ku grew, he separated the earth and sky. Each day he grew about ten feet, and the world and the heavens grew ten feet farther apart. When he stopped growing the distance between the earth and sky was set—90,000 *li* or 30,000 miles.

Based on an image of Sirius the Heavenly Wolf, from a Han dynasty container.

105

When P'an Ku died, his skull became the top of the sky, his blood ran in the rivers, his flesh turned into soil, his breath the wind, his voice thunder, his legs and arms the four directions. When he died, a large vacuum formed in the universe; pain and sin came into the world for the first time. The ancient Chinese believed that all that is *is* P'an Ku.

PROPPING UP THE SKY

Nü Kua, the Goddess of the River, with the body of a human being and the tail of a serpentine dragon, glided along the waters. She admired the beautiful forms made from the body of P'an Ku. She loved the trees and plants but was most fascinated with the livelier, more active animals and fish. She decided to create human beings from the mud on the riverbed. When her creatures were fully formed with arms, legs, and a head, she helped them to settle in villages and farms.

But these first people were soon threatened with destruction. The angry monster Gong-gong slammed his head against one of the great Chinese mountains, Mount Buzhou. The sky tumbled downward, and the Huang Ho River, nicknamed "China's Sorrow," overflowed its banks, and ruined the crops of poor Chinese farmers. Hundreds of Nü Kua's creations went hungry, starved to death, or drowned.

The Goddess was determined to protect them. To support the world roof, she sacrificed a giant tortoise. She propped each of its four gargantuan legs against the sky. The four columns mapped out the four directions—north, south, east, and west—for the earth, the ancient Chinese believed, is square with four corners. The universe is round, encircling the world and appearing to all Nü Kua's creations as a domed canopy.

The Expanding Universe
of Contemporary Science

Imagine a tiny point into which all that was to become the universe is tightly packed.

THE UNIVERSE OF CONTEMPORARY SCIENCE began with the Big Bang, an explosion that created the universe 12 to 15 billion years ago.

In Chinese mythology, the God P'an Ku curled inside an egg. When it hatched, P'an Ku created the universe by growing larger and larger. The taller P'an Ku became, the higher the heavens rose. Like the ancient Chinese, scientists now suggest that the universe began with all matter and energy contained within a kind of "cosmic egg," a tiny point with all of the elements that were to become the universe squeezed into it. Then, the Big Bang occurred. The "egg" blew apart. The universe expanded like the Chinese P'an Ku—matter and energy pushed outward in all directions, creating a larger and larger universe as it spread apart.

We can compare the Chinese belief in P'an Ku to the Big Bang. But is it fair to say that scientists believe in the Big Bang? Not exactly. Myths are different from science. The myths that are part of religious beliefs don't change. They are not tested—accepted or rejected according to measurable results. Myths are simply forgotten or replaced by other beliefs over time. Scientists say their observations are, at this state of our knowledge, best explained by an elemental burst. For scientists, knowledge is based on experiments, not on unquestioned beliefs. We like to think of the Big Bang as the scientific theory about Creation. But scientists don't think of the Big Bang as Creation. As E. C. Krupp, the director of the Griffith Observatory in Los Angeles, put it, the Big Bang is the time when the observed cosmos began behaving as we now observe it to behave.

Turn on a light in your room. The brightness appears instantaneously. But experiments have shown that light takes time to travel. It travels at about 186,282 miles per second. For us to see the stars, light has to travel the full distance from those fiery orbs to our eyes, where they appear as twinkling dots.

When we look out into the universe, we are actually looking backward in time. Looking at the sun, we are actually seeing a postcard from the sun sent to us about eight minutes ago. As we gaze at the center of the Milky Way Galaxy, we are looking toward the stars as they were 27,000 years ago. When we use powerful computers and telescopes to look at the farthest objects they can detect, we are actually looking at things that happened billions of years ago. Our most powerful telescopes can see a significant fraction of the way back to the Big Bang. Scientists have conducted experiments with microscopic particles to re-create what the universe was like a few seconds after the explosion.

They can also detect when a star in the universe burns out and collapses. As that happens, its gravity increases to a point that even light cannot get out. This phenomenon is what scientists call a *black hole.*

Some scientists also speculate about *wormholes* in the universe. According to some theories, a rocket plunging into a tunnel-like wormhole may crop up at a different place in the universe, a different point in time, or a parallel universe. These black holes and wormholes have led some scientists to speculate on the existence of other dimensions in the universe.

Flatland and a Universe of Many Dimensions

Although today's scientists don't tell tales about Gods and heroes, they often use stories and parables to convey their theories to the public. They are fond of talking about the imaginary universe depicted in a novel written by Edwin Abbott in 1884. He called his book *Flatland,* the same name as his fictional universe.

The characters in *Flatland* are a group of squares, lines, triangles, and circles. They live in a world with no height—flat as a page. As a consequence, the characters cannot picture what things look like in our three-dimensional universe.

One day, a sphere rolled across their world. The hero, Mr. Square, couldn't see the sphere because he lived in two dimensions—but as the sphere moved through his world as if it were passing through a piece of paper, Mr. Square saw a circle that grew bigger and then smaller. He began to suspect that something strange was happening.

In the novel, Sphere is a character from a different universe called Spaceland. He tried to explain what he looked like to Flatland's Mr. Square. He asked him to picture a direction that was "upward and not north-ward."

Mr. Square remained unconvinced of Sphere's existence. Suddenly, Mr. Square found himself peeled off Flatland and whirled into space.

Returned to the earth, he was finally persuaded. Mr. Square was so convinced, in fact, that he tried to convert his fellow Flatlanders to the idea of a third dimension. They labeled him a heretic and promptly threw him in jail.

Abbott's novel suggests how our own universe may have dimensions that we cannot see and therefore regard as inconceivable. Scientists sometimes refer to the novel as they try to convince us that the universe may exist in more than three dimensions.

By providing three numbers, we can find any point in our three-dimensional universe. If we want to meet someone for lunch in New York, we might say, "Meet me on the twenty-fourth floor of the building at the corner of Forty-second Street and First Avenue." Two numbers give us the corner, the third the height.

Many current scientists, from Albert Einstein onward, suggest that time is a fourth dimension. If we want to meet someone for lunch, we must also specify the time—let's say 12:30 P.M. Thus, we give ourselves a fourth dimension. We don't think of time as a dimension because, unlike length, width, and height, time is something we are living through. *Time* is unlike the other dimensions; we can measure it, but we can't see it. Contemporary physicists such as Edward Witten and Stephen Hawking speculate that black holes and wormholes—along with some of the smallest particles in the universe—suggest the existence of still other dimensions to the universe that we are now only beginning to comprehend.

Alice in Wonderland: A Looking Glass of Microscopes and Telescopes

In Lewis Carroll's stories about Alice in Wonderland, Alice eats a cookie that says "Eat me" to become very, very big and drinks from a bottle that says "Drink me" to become very, very small. Alice is like the scientists in that she found a way to explore the large and small in her universe, Wonderland. Today's scientists, like Alice, have found the means to explore the immense and the minute. They use powerful telescopes to examine the largest objects and to measure the farthest distances in the universe; and they use microscopes and nuclear equipment to study the universe's tiniest particles, which are smaller than atoms and are called *quanta.*

In what was perhaps the most remarkable set of discoveries in all of history, Einstein, in the early twentieth century, came up with a series of insights about the universe just by thinking about his observations. He realized, for instance, that nothing could ever travel faster than the speed of light because at those high speeds, time itself would slow down. From that key observation, he determined that time is a dimension of the universe like length, width, and height. This idea came to be known as the *special theory of relativity.*

Although Isaac Newton first calculated the rules of gravity in the seventeenth century, no one had been able to figure out precisely how the force of gravity worked. We knew that the mass of the earth kept us on the planet, and the mass of the sun kept the earth in orbit. Einstein's later *general theory of relativity* showed that the mass of an object actually curves space itself, and the curving is what causes gravity. Scientists compared this to the effect a bowling ball would have on a small marble that is placed on a thin rubber sheet. The bowling ball would sink and bend the sheet so that the marble would tend to roll around and toward it. The curve on the sheet helps illustrate the way the mass of the sun curves space so that the earth revolves around it. Einstein conceptualized the idea of *space-time* and a universe that is very different from what we see as we look out into the night sky.

At the same time Einstein was working on his theories, a group of other scientists were exploring the world of submicroscopic particles. They discovered effects that are as odd as anything Alice discovered in Wonderland. On this almost unimaginably small level, the units scientists study are so tiny that the very act of defining exactly where they are changes them. A famous scientist named Werner Heisenberg finally decided that all we can do is define the probability that a unit might be in one place or another. We have to accept an ultimate uncertainty about exactly what is so at a given moment.

When speaking about this most basic subatomic level, the rules that govern the world we can see and touch change. Like Alice, scientists have to make sense of what they observe even if it is unlike anything they ever knew before.

Most recently, scientists are struggling to put what they have learned from studying submicroscopic particles together with Einstein's theories about stars and vast distances in space. Scientists are seeking a unified theory that can explain both sets of ideas. Some have put forward what they call a *string theory,* which suggests that all matter, small and large, is put together of small vibrating strings. Many scientists hope that this idea will be able to explain, for instance, the Big Bang, a time when the universe, which was soon to be very big, was very small.

The ideas of contemporary science paint a picture of the universe that is as interesting and unusual as the Iroquois notion of the world as a turtle, or the Chinese idea of the cosmic egg. In our time, we have been able to use powerful telescopes to explore galaxies, black holes, microscopic particles, and the Big Bang; but in a thousand years, our ideas may look completely different. Human beings living then may look back at our views as one more picture of the universe hanging in the gallery of wondrous cosmologies that people have used to explain where we are in the universe, and how we came to be here. Scientists of a later time will be able to see farther into space and look deeper into the tiniest particles. They will devise amazing cosmologies—because they have our shoulders to stand on.

CONCLUSION

At different times in human history, on different continents, this planet and its surroundings have seemed a very different place—a giant turtle, a huge brain, a calabash, a world tree, or the creation of a single God. The earth and sky have held each other in a close embrace or been packed together in a cosmic egg. Scientists have gone from thinking of the earth as the center of the universe to a planet revolving around a small star in a distant corner of the galaxy.

Yet, for all of these differences in how we see the world, a common bond unites us as human beings—a passionate desire to understand the universe and our place in it. Some scientists have even wondered if we were put on this planet because the universe needed a way to understand itself.

In ancient Scandinavian mythology, the earth Goddess Frigg bends over the world loom. The spindle of her spinning wheel faces north, along the axis around which the sky turns each night. Her loom is lined out east to west along the celestial equator. Turning the earth and sky, she spins the thread of time. At her task, she suggests the beautiful way that ancient myths interpret the world and the mysteries of science as they unravel the secrets of time. At her loom our day-to-day lives are woven and worn even as we try to understand and appreciate the vivid patterns of our universe, which snugly surrounds and touches us. What a beautiful cloak she weaves!

Source Notes

Introduction

The ideas in my introduction are drawn from some of the classic works that have also inspired this book: Carl Sagan's book *Cosmos*, Charles J. Caes's *Cosmology: The Search for the Order of the Universe*, and E. C. Krupp's *Beyond the Blue Horizon: Myths and Legends of the Sun, Moon, Stars, and Planets* (the wonderful story about Rabba bar Bar-Hana, for instance, is from Krupp).

The categories around which the book is structured are inspired in part by the categorization of origin myths set forth in David and Margaret Leeming's *A Dictionary of Creation Myths*. A useful introduction to the stories from world mythology is Donna Rosenberg's *World Mythology: An Anthology of the Great Myths and Epics*.

For this book, I have tried to go back as closely as possible to the primary sources and their translations.

According to Raphael Patai, *cosmogony* is a term first used by the Greek writer Plutarch (46–120 C.E.) to describe the theories that explained the origin of the universe. *Cosmology* was a term used in 1730 by Christian Wolff, a famous German philosopher and mathematician.

The Maori Cosmos

Anyone interested in the wonderful myths of the Maori should read the version by Sir George Grey, who first collected them. He issued the book first as *Nga mahi a nga tupuna* (*The Deeds of the Ancestors*) in 1854. He then translated it into English under the title: *Polynesian Mythology and Ancient Traditional History of the Maori as Told by Their Priests and Chiefs.* It was first published in 1855. William W. Bird edited a new edition, published in New Zealand in 1956. Two useful retellings of these stories can be found in Antony Alpers's *Maori Myths and Tribal Legends,* and A. W. Reed's *Maori Myth: The Supernatural World of the Maori.*

The Egyptian Cosmos

Egyptian civilization flourished for almost three thousand years, and the stories of Gods and Goddesses changed dramatically during that period. The earliest known inscriptions from Egyptian mythology date from as early as 2345 B.C.E. At that time, when a king died, he was entombed within a pyramid. Stories of Gods and Goddesses were inscribed in hieroglyphic writing on the walls. These are called the *Pyramid Texts* (the creation story and the genealogy of the Gods are referred to in these texts). Later, when it was no longer possible to create a pyramid for every king, the stories were inscribed on coffins. The inscriptions from this period are called the *Coffin Texts*. Later, mythological stories were written on papyrus (a form of early paper) and put inside the coffins as scrolls. In addition to the inscriptions from these three periods, much is known about Egyptian myths from later Greek and Roman writers who translated ancient Egyptians texts that have since been destroyed.

The story I've called "Eye of the Sun" is from a papyrus script (Twentieth Dynasty, 1200–1085 B.C.E.). The source for much of my research were the volumes by E. A. Wallis Budge, *The Egyptian Book of the Dead* and *The Gods of the Egyptians*. Budge was the keeper of Assyrian and Egyptian antiquities in the British Museum in the late nineteenth and early twentieth centuries, and his books provide the original hieroglyphic texts as well as translation and interpretation.

I have also drawn on some secondary source material, including Virginia Hamilton's *In the Beginning* (which includes the boat called *Millions of Years*), Veronica Ions's *Egyptian Mythology*, and Donna Rosenberg's, *World Mythology: An Anthology of the Great Myths and Epics*.

The Greek Cosmos

Hesiod's *Theogony* stands with Homer's classics, the *Iliad* and *Odyssey*, at the beginning of the Western literary tradition. *Theogony* is a beautiful epic poem, told far more beautifully by Hesiod in poetry than by the many students of mythology who have retold the story in prose. My quote from *Theogony* is from Hesiod, *Works and Days and Theogony*, translated by Stanley Lombardo in 1993. Hesiod's creation myth is one of four creation myths in ancient Greek mythology. Good retellings can be found in Edith Hamilton's classic *Mythology: Timeless Tales of Gods and Heroes* and Donna Rosenberg's *World Mythology*.

The Hebrew Cosmos

For this version I have drawn upon Sandol Stoddard's *The Doubleday Illustrated Children's Bible*, with paintings by Tony Chen, as well as on the King James Bible. The Jewish Torah, or Bible, later became the Old Testament for Christians. The New Testament told the stories about the birth, death, and resurrection of Jesus. Some scholars have noted that the Christians added an additional mythological element by introducing Jesus, the son of God, who walked on the earth. Unlike the Old Testament, which concentrates on historical legends about men and women, the New Testament relates stories about the son of God.

The Hindu Cosmos

The oldest Hindu creation stories come from the *Rig Veda,* the first of the four Vedas composed by invaders who came into India from Iran in the second millennium B.C.E. Other creation stories followed in the *Upanishads* between 800 and 400 B.C.E. The stories in the introduction to this section are from the *Puranas* (old stories) from 300 B.C.E.

A useful, simple retelling of some of the stories and descriptions of the Gods, and my source for much of this section, is a book called *Hindu Deities* by Swami Jagdishwaranand, published by the Geeta Temple in Elmhurst, Queens. The passage from the "Hymn to Vishnu" is from "The Indian Song of Songs" in Edwin Arnold's *Indian Poetry* published in 1884.

The story of the eclipse and Rahu appears in Krupp's excellent book *Beyond the Blue Horizon.* It is originally from the *Mahabharata,* the great epic poem of India. One of the world's longest literary works, it is a primary source of Hindu mythology. It was first written down in the early fifth century B.C.E., and it continues to be expanded to this day. Stories from it currently appear in movies, puppet theaters, and even comic books of modern New Delhi and Bombay.

The Norse Cosmos

Although the most learned Norsemen of northern Europe could carve runic letters on wood or stone, they did not write down their tales and myths. Fortunately, poets continued to pass them down through the oral tradition until Christianity brought with it the art of writing on parchment with a pen. By the twelfth century, Christianity was firmly rooted in northern Europe, and the monks and religious leaders no longer feared a return to paganism. Around the year 1220, when the old Norse stories were beginning to fade from men's minds, the gifted historian, politician, and poet Snorri Sturluson wrote them down in what has come to be called the *Prose Edda,* from which the stories in this book were taken. The passage I quote about the end of the world is from Chapter 51, and my source is the 1847 volume *Northern Antiquities* by Paul Henri Mallet, translated from the French and with notes by Bishop Percy. A fine retelling of the stories that inspired my work is H. R. Ellis Davidson's *Gods and Myths of Northern Europe.*

The Cosmos of Early Western Science

One of my great pleasures in writing this volume was to revisit Carl Sagan's beautifully written book *Cosmos,* based on his thirteen-part television series. Two other useful books were Charles J. Caes's *Cosmology: The Search for the Order of the Universe* and Edward Grant's *Planets, Stars & Orbs: The Medieval Cosmos 1200–1687*. An excellent scientific overview of early cosmologies appears in the *Dictionary of the History of Ideas*, published by Scribner, with Philip Wiener as its editor in chief.

The ideas of Copernicus in the sixteenth century were foreshadowed by the scientist Aristarchus in the third century B.C.E., whose ideas were dismissed in his own day. He believed that the earth spun on its axis each day and that the stars remained motionless. He also computed that the sun is about three hundred times larger than the earth. So how could such a big mass revolve around such a small one? It couldn't, he reasoned—the earth must revolve around the sun.

The Inca Cosmos

For this section, I have focused on how the Incas built their great highways to reflect their perception of the Milky Way. But the Incas also worshiped the sun, and there are many other ways in which Incan architecture was constructed to utilize the sun and stars. Two good books to explore the mythology of the Incas are Michael E. Moseley's *Incas and Their Ancestors: The Archaeology of Peru* and John Bierhorst's *The Mythology of South America*. An interesting essay about the relationship of astronomy and architecture in the Incan, Aztec, and Mayan cultures appeared in the *National Geographic* essay "America's Ancient Skywatchers" by John B. Carlson, with pictures by Bob Sacha, published in March 1990.

There are many variants of the Incan Creation story about the rod of gold. The most influential is from Garcilaso de la Vega in his *Royal Commentaries of the Incas* published in 1609. He was the son of a Spanish soldier and an Incan princess and wrote from his memory of stories he heard as a child from an uncle on his mother's side.

The Jain Cosmos

For this brief section on the Jains, I have drawn on Joseph Campbell's *The Masks of God: Oriental Mythology*, as well as on David and Margaret Leeming's *A Dictionary of Creation Myths*. Other useful treatments include Sinclair Stevenson's *The Heart of Jainism* and Heinrich Zimmer's *Philosophies of India*.

The Desana Cosmos

I am grateful to E. C. Krupp's *Beyond the Blue Horizon*, which led me to the essay "Brain and Mind in Desana Shamanism" by anthropologist G. Reichel-Dolmatoff in the *Journal of Latin American Lore*, published in 1981. As an anthropologist in the Amazon region, Reichel-

Dolmatoff worked extensively with shamans, medicine men, healers, and mystics of the area's Indian tribes.

The Haitian Cosmos

My initial source for this section was *The Divine Horsemen: The Living Gods of Haiti* by Maya Deren. The author was a filmmaker who first visited Haiti in 1947. In one chapter of her compelling book, she describes what it is like to become possessed by the Gods in Haiti.

I've also been deeply inspired by the ethnomusicologist and my close friend Lois Wilcken, who has been documenting and writing about Vodou culture for more than a decade and who read and reread the Haitian portion of this manuscript. In recent years, a stunning exhibition on Haitian arts has been touring the United States, and the catalog to the exhibit, *Sacred Arts of Haitian Vodou,* is an excellent guided tour through Haitian Vodou culture.

The Iroquois Cosmos

I am grateful to Abenaki poet and storyteller Joseph Bruchac who led me to several early sources of this well-known story. In the nineteenth century, Tuscarora Indian writer David Cusick wrote down an early version of this Creation story. Reverend William M. Beauchamp published it in his volume *Iroquois Trail* in

1892, which contains many of Cusick's stories. I also drew on Arthur C. Parker's *Seneca Myths and Legends*, originally published in 1923. Finally, I drew on Jeremiah Curtin's *Seneca Indian Myths*, also published in 1923. Curtin worked for the pioneering Bureau of Ethnology of the Smithsonian Institution and took down the stories in their original form as told to him by aged Indians of the Seneca tribe. I have tried to incorporate some of the original language of these early versions in my own retelling of the story.

The Fon Cosmos

The Dahomean Creation story was recorded by Melville J. and Frances S. Herskovits in 1931. Most of the storytellers were older men, many of them priests of cults or cult members. In the cities of Abomey, Allada, and Whydah, the two anthropologists hired interpreters. The native people would tell their tales, and the Herskovitses would take them down on a typewriter. Their book *Dahomean Narrative* was published in 1958.

The Chumash Cosmos

My source for this section is *December's Child: A Book of Chumash Oral Narratives*, edited and with an analysis by Thomas C. Blackburn. This study, originally Blackburn's doctoral dissertation, draws on the work of the eccentric ethnologist and linguist John Peabody Harrington. Although he left behind a lifetime of work in more than four hundred large boxes at the Smithsonian Institution, he published very little in his lifetime.

One of his chief informants, María Solarez, was born at Mission Santa Ynez and lived in the Santa Ynez Valley for most of her life. She was one the most knowledgeable people he interviewed about the older Chumash myths. The stories of María Solarez have been slightly edited. She refers to Sun's partner with a Chumash term that in English employs arcane diacritical symbols no lay reader could understand. Scholars have suggested she is referring to the evening star, and I have used Evening Star instead of her term in the story.

The Chinese Cosmos

The Chinese myths current today are not as ancient as the culture. In ancient China, many books existed in only one copy. In 213 B.C.E. the first emperor of China burned all books that were not about farming, medicine, prophecy, or raising trees and plants. During the great Han dynasty (206 B.C.E.–220 C.E.), many of the old stories that were still told in oral tradition were written down again. The Creation story about P'an Ku is the most detailed of the Chinese Creation myths and appeared in popular legend as well as a third-century literary text called *San-wu li-chi*.

The Chinese Creation stories appear in Donna Rosenberg's *World Mythology*, the Leemings' *A Dictionary of*

Creation Myths, and Barbara Sproul's *Primal Myths: Creation Myths Around the World.*

The Cosmos of Contemporary Science

Throughout the twentieth century, the work of theoretical physicists, beginning with Albert Einstein, opened up a universe filled with the same wonder and awe as any of the ancient myths. The key contemporary scientific theories about the universe, including the theory of relativity, the uncertainty principle, string theory, and the Big Bang, are based on complex mathematical calculations that are, in turn, based on observations into the distant universe and the tiniest particles. Yet, we are lucky to have a number of fine scientist/writers who have written books for the general public. Anyone interested in contemporary science should pick up some of these: *Cosmos* by Carl Sagan, *Hyperspace* by Michio Kaku, *The Dancing Wu Li Masters* by Gary Zukav. An excellent, easy-to-understand book on both relativity, quantum theory, and string theory is Brian Greene's *The Elegant Universe.* I am grateful to Carl Sagan's book for comparing the Big Bang theories to some of the ancient myths of the "Cosmic Egg."

AUTHOR'S NOTE

From the first idea to the final draft, I have relished the task of writing this book. Youngsters are a wonderful audience for these stories because they marvel at the connections among these ancient myths and ideas. Yet, comparative studies have become an unpopular subject for many folklorists and anthropologists. With the notable exception of Joseph Campbell, who wrote for the general public rather than a scholarly audience, there are few recent scholars who have undertaken the work of comparing cultural forms such as myths and legends.

Folklorists and anthropologists have come to believe that cultures are so different from one another that the only studies that make sense are in-depth explorations of single cultures. Comparing myths and stories over vast periods of time and space has its pitfalls. But by avoiding comparison, we lose an opportunity to explore and wonder at the commonalities and differences with which we as human beings, living on and looking at the same world, express our deepest ideas about who we are. We lose a chance to appreciate human experience in its broadest form. I have tried to express the wondrous similarities and differences in world cosmologies in this book. My hope is that it will inspire a younger generation to never lose sight of the big picture as they seek to understand their place in the world.

FOR FURTHER READING

Alpers, Antony. *Maori Myths and Tribal Legends*. London: John Murray, 1964.

Arnold, Edwin. *Indian Poetry*. London: Trübner & Co., Ludgate Hill, 1884.

Beauchamp, William Martin. *The Iroquois Trail; or, Footprints of the Six Nations in Customs, Traditions, and History by W. M. Beauchamp; in Which Are Included David Cusick's Sketches of Ancient History of the Six Nations*. Fayetteville, NY: H. C. Beauchamp, 1892. Reprint, New York: AMS Press, 1976.

Bierhorst, John. *The Mythology of Mexico and Central America*. New York: William Morrow and Company, 1990.

———. *The Mythology of South America*. New York: William Morrow and Company, 1988.

Blackburn, Thomas C., ed. *December's Child: A Book of Chumash Oral Narratives*. Berkeley: University of California Press, 1975.

Bruchac, Joseph and Jonathan London. *Thirteen Moons on Turtle's Back: A Native American Year of Moons*. Illustrated by Thomas Locker. New York: Philomel Books, The Putnam and Grosset Group, 1992.

Budge, E. A. Wallis. *The Egyptian Book of the Dead and the Papyrus of Ani*.

New York: G.P. Putnam's Sons, 1894. Reprint, Brooklyn, NY: A&B, 1999.

Budge, E. A. Wallis. *The Gods of the Egyptians; or, Studies in Egyptian Mythology.* New York: Dover, 1969.

Caes, Charles J. *Cosmology: The Search for the Order of the Universe.* Blue Ridge Summit, PA: Tab Books Inc., 1986.

Carlson, John B. "America's Ancient Skywatchers." Photographs by Bob Sacha. *National Geographic* 177:3 (March 1990).

Curtin, Jeremiah. *Seneca Indian Myths.* New York: E. P. Dutton, 1923.

Davidson, H. R. Ellis. *Gods and Myths of Northern Europe.* Baltimore: Penguin Books, 1964.

Deren, Maya. *Divine Horsemen: The Living Gods of Haiti.* Originally published in London: Thames and Hudson, 1953. Reprint, Kingston, NY: McPherson & Co., 1970.

Greene, Brian. *The Elegant Universe: Superstrings, Hidden Dimensions, and the Quest for the Ultimate Theory.* New York: W.W. Norton & Company, 1999.

Grey, Sir George. *Polynesian Mythology and Ancient Traditional History of the Maori as Told by Their Priests and Chiefs.* Ed. William W. Bird. Auckland: Whitcombe and Tombs, 1956.

Hamilton, Edith. *Mythology: Timeless Tales of Gods and Heroes.* New York: The New American Library of World Literature, Inc., 1953.

Johnson, Elias. *Legends, Traditions and Laws of the Iroquois, or Six Nations, and History of the Tuscarora Indians.* Lockport, NY: Union Printing and Publishing Company, 1881.

Kaku, Michio. *Hyperspace: A Scientific Odyssey Through Parallel Universes, Time Warps, and the Tenth Dimension.* New York: Oxford University Press, 1994.

Krupp, E. C. *Beyond the Blue Horizon: Myths and Legends of the Sun, Moon, Stars and Planets.* New York: Oxford University Press, 1991.

Leeming, David and Margaret Leeming. *A Dictionary of Creation Myths.* New York: Oxford University Press, 1994.

Moseley, Michael E. *The Incas and Their Ancestors: The Archaeology of Peru.* London: Thames and Hudson, 1992.

Pannekoek, A. *A History of Astronomy.* London: George Allen & Unwin, 1961.

Parker, Arthur C. *Seneca Myths and Legends.* Originally published in New York: Buffalo Historical Society, 1923. Reprint, with introduction by William N. Fenton, in Lincoln, NE: University of Nebraska Press, 1989.

Philip, Neil. *The Illustrated Book of Myths: Tales and Legends of the World.* Illustrated by Nilesh Mistry. London: Dorling Kindersley, 1995.

Rosenberg, Donna. *World Mythology: An Anthology of the Great Myths and Epics.* Chicago: Passport Books, National Textbook Company, 1986.

Sagan, Carl. *Cosmos.* New York: Random House, 1980.

Stoddard, Sandol. *The Doubleday Illustrated Children's Bible.* Illustrated by Tony Chen. New York: Doubleday, 1983.

San Rafael High School Library
185 Mission Avenue
San Rafael, CA 94901